Green Finance and Investment

AF706567

Climate Adaptation Investment Framework

OECD

BETTER POLICIES FOR BETTER LIVES

This work is published under the responsibility of the Secretary-General of the OECD. The opinions expressed and arguments employed herein do not necessarily reflect the official views of the Member countries of the OECD.

This document, as well as any data and map included herein, are without prejudice to the status of or sovereignty over any territory, to the delimitation of international frontiers and boundaries and to the name of any territory, city or area.

The statistical data for Israel are supplied by and under the responsibility of the relevant Israeli authorities. The use of such data by the OECD is without prejudice to the status of the Golan Heights, East Jerusalem and Israeli settlements in the West Bank under the terms of international law.

Note by the Republic of Türkiye
The information in this document with reference to "Cyprus" relates to the southern part of the Island. There is no single authority representing both Turkish and Greek Cypriot people on the Island. Türkiye recognises the Turkish Republic of Northern Cyprus (TRNC). Until a lasting and equitable solution is found within the context of the United Nations, Türkiye shall preserve its position concerning the "Cyprus issue".

Note by all the European Union Member States of the OECD and the European Union
The Republic of Cyprus is recognised by all members of the United Nations with the exception of Türkiye. The information in this document relates to the area under the effective control of the Government of the Republic of Cyprus.

Please cite this publication as:
OECD (2024), *Climate Adaptation Investment Framework*, Green Finance and Investment, OECD Publishing, Paris, https://doi.org/10.1787/8686fc27-en.

ISBN 978-92-64-99896-4 (print)
ISBN 978-92-64-51365-5 (PDF)
ISBN 978-92-64-39189-5 (HTML)

Green Finance and Investment
ISSN 2409-0336 (print)
ISSN 2409-0344 (online)

Revised version, February 2025
Details of revisions available at: https://www.oecd.org/en/publications/support/corrigenda.html

Photo credits: Cover © marcin jucha/shutterstock.com

Corrigenda to OECD publications may be found at: https://www.oecd.org/en/publications/support/corrigenda.html.
© OECD 2024

Attribution 4.0 International (CC BY 4.0)
This work is made available under the Creative Commons Attribution 4.0 International licence. By using this work, you accept to be bound by the terms of this licence (https://creativecommons.org/licenses/by/4.0/).
Attribution – you must cite the work.
Translations – you must cite the original work, identify changes to the original and add the following text: *In the event of any discrepancy between the original work and the translation, only the text of original work should be considered valid.*
Adaptations – you must cite the original work and add the following text: *This is an adaptation of an original work by the OECD. The opinions expressed and arguments employed in this adaptation should not be reported as representing the official views of the OECD or of its Member countries.*
Third-party material – the licence does not apply to third-party material in the work. If using such material, you are responsible for obtaining permission from the third party and for any claims of infringement.
You must not use the OECD logo, visual identity or cover image without express permission or suggest the OECD endorses your use of the work.
Any dispute arising under this licence shall be settled by arbitration in accordance with the Permanent Court of Arbitration (PCA) Arbitration Rules 2012. The seat of arbitration shall be Paris (France). The number of arbitrators shall be one.

Foreword

A significant increase in investment in climate change adaptation is needed to build resilience to the current and future impacts of climate change. There is a strong economic case for doing so, particularly given that investments in adaptation can deliver multiple benefits. For example, green roofs can reduce energy costs, reduce stormwater runoff and contribute to biodiversity. Similarly, integrating climate-resilience into infrastructure design can reduce maintenance costs and increase reliability, while also reducing losses if an extreme event occurs.

Governments have a key role in unlocking this potential by putting in place a policy framework that provides the right signals to encourage investment in adaptation. Achieving this will require enhanced coherence and coordination between all parts of government. Climate adaptation is usually the responsibility of environment ministries, but critical policies for influencing investment in adaptation are the responsibility of finance and other sectoral ministries. Improving coordination and addressing policy misalignments and gaps can encourage investment in adaptation.

The Climate Adaptation Investment Framework has been developed to assist governments in creating a conducive policy enabling environment for investment in adaptation. It has been developed as a collaboration between the OECD'S Environment Policy and Investment Committees. Building on the OECD's Policy Framework for Investment (PFI) and FDI Qualities Policy Toolkit, it identifies six key policy areas ("building blocks") for increasing investment in climate change adaptation. These policy areas include strategic planning, public finance and investment and support for private investment. Each building block includes examples of international good practice, diagnostic questions and links to further resources.

This Framework is non-prescriptive and flexible, reflecting the context-specific nature of climate impacts and differences between countries' priorities, financial resources and capacities, including the specific challenges faced by developing countries. Rather than setting out a fixed agenda for reform, it provides policy makers with a set of questions to ask about the policy environment as part of the process of setting priorities and identifying potential areas for reform. It can be used for self-evaluation by countries, as part of peer-review processes or as a basis for dialogue between the public and private sectors.

Acknowledgements

This report is a joint output from the OECD's Directorate for Financial and Enterprise Affairs and the Environment Directorate. It contributes to the work programmes of the Environment Policy Committee (EPOC) and the Investment Committee (IC). It was co-authored by Michael Mullan and Iris Mantovani, with valuable contributions from Konstantin Blondeau. This work was undertaken under the guidance of Robert Youngman and Yuval Laster (Environment Directorate) and Martin Wermelinger and Ana Novik (Directorate for Financial and Enterprise Affairs). It was prepared for publication by Elvira Berrueta-Imaz.

The authors would like to thank the following OECD colleagues for their valuable advice and suggestions on previous drafts of this report. Mikaela Rambali, Simon Touboul, Sophie Lavaud, Geraldine Ang, Valentina Belessi, Leigh Wolfrom, Mamiko Yokoi-Arai, Sophia Gnych, Wiebke Bartz-Zuccala, Emilia Stazi, Kerstin Schopohl, Emma Raiteri and Ada Ignaciuk.

The OECD Environment Policy Committee (EPOC) and Investment Committee (IC) were responsible for oversight of this report. The Working Party on Finance and Investment for Environmental Goals (WPFIEG), the Working Party on Climate Change (WPCC) and the FDI Qualities Policy Network provided valuable feedback on previous drafts, alongside the Informal Expert Group that was established to support this project. The Framework has benefitted from the comments and suggestions of: Arghya Sinha Roy (Asian Development Bank), Vladimir Stenek (IFC), Jia Li and Chloe Desjonqueres (World Bank), Paul Smith and Gary Power (UNEP-FI), Craig Davies (Cadlas), Kit England (PWA Associates), Raffaele Della Croce (Imperial) and Jennifer Doherty (IADB).

This report has benefitted from the financial support of Japan, Environment and Climate Change Canada and the United States, as well as from the governments of the Netherlands and Switzerland through their support to the FDI Qualities Implementation Roadmap.

Table of contents

FIGURES

TABLES

BOXES

Abbreviations and acronyms

ADB	Asian Development Bank
AI	Artificial Intelligence
ARIC	Adaptation and Resilience Investors Collaborative
BII	British International Investment
BIS	Bank for International Settlement
C3S	Copernicus Climate Change Service
CAIF	Climate Adaptation Investment Framework
CAIP	Climate Adaptation Investment Planning
CBI	Climate Bonds Initiative
CCC	The United Kingdom's Climate Change Committee
CFMCA	Coalition of Finance Ministers for Climate Action
CO-WY	Colorado-Wyoming
CPI	Climate Policy Initiative
DNP	Department of National Planning
EBRD	European Bank for Reconstruction and Development
ECB	European Central Bank
EIB	European Investment Bank
EMDEs	Emerging markets and developing economies
FAO	Food and Agriculture Organization.
FDI	Foreign Direct Investment
FMO	FMO Netherlands Development Finance Company
FONERWA	Rwanda Green Fund
GCEW	Global Commission on the Economics of Water
GCF	Green Climate Fund
GCOS	Global Climate Observing System
GEF	Global Environment Facility
GEO	Group on Earth Observation
GFT	Green Finance Taxonomy
GIF	Global Infrastructure Facility
GIZ	German Agency for International Cooperation (Deutsche Gesellschaft für Internationale Zusammenarbeit)
Gov4Res	Governance for Resilient Development in the Pacific programme
GSSS	Green, social, sustainability and sustainability-linked bonds

I4CE	Institute for Climate Economics
IBRD	International Bank for Reconstruction and Development
IDB	Inter-American Development Bank
IFC	International Finance Corporation
IFRS	International Financial Reporting Standards
IPAs	Investment promotion agencies
IPCC	Intergovernmental Panel on Climate Change
IRA	Inflation Reduction Act
IsDB	Islamic Development Bank
ISO	International Organization for Standardization
ISSB	International Sustainability Standards Board
JICA	Japan International Cooperation Agency
MAFF	Japan's Ministry of Agriculture, Food and Fisheries
MAR	Mesoamerican Reef
NAPs	National Adaptation Plans
NCA	Natural Capital Accounting
NCQG	New Quantified Collective Goal
NDCs	Nationally Determined Contributions
NFIP	National Flood Insurance Program
NOAA	National Oceanic and Atmospheric Administration
NWFE	Nexus of Water, Food and Energy Programme
OECD	Organisation for Economic Co-operation and Development
PFI	Policy Framework for Investment
PIDG	Private Infrastructure Development Group
PPFs	Project preparation facilities
PPPs	Public-Private Partnerships
SLBs	Sustainability-linked bonds
SME	Small or Medium-sized Enterprise
TCFD	Task Force on Climate Related Financial Disclosures
UNDP	United Nations Development Programme
UNDRR	United Nations International Strategy for Disaster Reduction
UNEP FI	United Nations Environment Programme Finance Initiative
UNFCCC	United Nations Framework Convention on Climate Change
WEF	World Economic Forum
WMO	World Meteorological Organization
WRI	World Resources Institute
WRMU	Water Resources Management Unit

Executive Summary

The Climate Adaptation Investment Framework (CAIF) aims to support governments' efforts to unlock investment in adaptation to build resilience to climate change. Building upon the foundation of the OECD's Policy Framework for Investment and the Foreign Direct Investment (FDI) Qualities Policy Toolkit, it identifies the key domestic policies that are particularly relevant for enabling climate change adaptation investment. The scope of the CAIF includes both public and private investment, given that both sources will be critical for climate adaptation.

The physical impacts of climate change are already being felt, with record-setting extreme heatwaves, droughts and wildfire. Losses from weather and climate-related disasters were USD 281 billion in that year, and mostly uninsured. Climate-related losses are projected to increase due to climate change, with extreme events become increasingly frequent and severe and slow-onset changes becoming increasingly evident. As the severity of these hazards increase, there is the risk of abrupt re-pricing and stranding of assets. A disorderly transition to growing physical climate risks would have grave socio-economic consequences, including on employment, health, productivity and public finances.

Increased public and private investment will be needed in activities that help to reduce harms or realise any potential opportunities due to the impacts of climate change ("adaptation investments"), such as the development of climate-resilient infrastructure, food systems and supply chains. Adaptation investments are economically and socially worthwhile. The benefits will be context specific, but there is a large volume of economically worthwhile investment opportunities: one study identified USD 1.8 trillion of adaptation investments, with benefit-cost ratios ranging from 2:1 to 10:1.

Despite this potential, investments are not yet occurring at scale, with recorded finance flows in the tens of billions of dollars and estimated needs in the hundreds of billions of dollars. This Framework identifies the domestic policies that can help to realise this potential, while recognising the importance of other areas of the enabling environment including capacity and domestic financial resources, particularly for developing countries. As such, it is intended to complement existing initiatives to strengthen capacity and increase developing countries' access to finance.

This Framework identifies the policies that are required to ensure that the benefits of enhanced resilience to climate change are visible and reflected in the allocation of public and private resources. In doing so, it aims to remove barriers to investment in adaptation by proposing a comprehensive approach to address market failures, correct misaligned policies and provide incentives for investments that deliver wider social benefits. International cooperation will be essential for supporting action in developing countries.

Strategic planning processes, including the development of National Adaptation Plans (NAPs) and Nationally Determined Contributions (NDCs), provide a key entry point for unlocking investment in adaptation. These processes have already made progress in identifying climate risks and mainstreaming into policy development, but there remain significant challenges in translating planning into action on the ground. This Framework has been designed to help governments and partners identify potential gaps in the policy enabling environment and identify the resources and good practices that can help to address those gaps. It is non-prescriptive and flexible, reflecting the context-specific nature of climate impacts and differences between countries' priorities, financial resources and capacities. It can be used for self-evaluation by countries, as part of peer-review processes or as an input into dialogues between the public and private sectors.

The Framework is arranged around six building blocks, identifying key policy areas for supporting investment in adaptation and addressing the following areas of good practice:

Building block	Key policy recommendations and good practices
Strategic planning and policy coherence	• Set clear objectives, metrics and targets in national adaptation planning documents. • Ensure close engagement in planning by central planning and sectoral ministries. • Assess economic consequences of climate change and needs for finance. • Clarify responsibilities for managing climate-related risks. • Translate adaptation priorities into a robust financing strategy, such as an adaptation investment plan. • Support the provision of reliable data on climate risks, for example through online climate data platforms. • Track progress in mobilising investment for adaptation.
Regulatory alignment	• Ensure that the regulatory framework for investment is transparent, predictable, and fair. • Reform distorting subsidies for agriculture. • Examine requirements for business continuity and health and safety. • Provide regulatory incentives for climate-resilient infrastructure. • Strengthen incentives for enhancing the natural environment and ecosystems. • Ensure water allocation regimes reward efficient use while meeting equity objectives. • Update technical codes and standards to ensure that they are suitable for the impacts of climate change. • Ensure that economic regulation of infrastructure networks is conducive to investment in adaptation.
Insurance and risk transfer	• Ensure that the policy framework for insurance is conducive to investment in risk reduction through pricing, terms and conditions. • Explore opportunities to encourage resilient recovery following extreme events through regulation or subsidies. • Support the uptake of insurance for climate-related risks, including through the deployment of innovative approaches such as parametric insurance.
Public finance and investment	• Ensure that the benefits of climate resilience are integrated into budgetary processes and project appraisals. • Implement public procurement policies that account for benefits over the lifecycle of the investment. • Ensure that climate risks are clearly identified and managed when undertaking public-private partnerships (PPPs). • Implement a strategy for managing the financial consequences to the public sector of climate extremes.
Sustainable finance	• Support the uptake of financial instruments for investment in adaptation by examining regulatory frameworks and, where appropriate, through issuance of these instruments by the public sector. • Support the uptake of credible and consistent standards, labels and taxonomies for identifying adaptation investments, whether through regulatory or voluntary approaches. • Examine financial regulation and supervision to ensure that physical climate risks are appropriately considered within the financial sector.
Support and incentives for private investment	• Consider the development of targeted incentives for private investments in adaptation that deliver social benefits. • Expand support for project development for adaptation investments, for example through project preparation facilities. • Examine the intellectual property framework to identify any potential barriers to investment in adaptation innovation. • Enhance support for innovation related to climate adaptation, such as technology centres, business incubators and applied research centres.

1 Introduction

This chapter provides the context for the Climate Adaptation Investment Framework. It outlines investment needs and opportunities for climate adaptation, provides key definitions and explains how this Framework links to the Policy Framework for Investment (PFI) and FDI Qualities policy toolkit. It also outlines how this Framework can be integrated into adaptation planning processes.

The Climate Adaptation Investment Framework (CAIF) identifies the policies that can enable increased public and private investment[1] in activities that help to build resilience to the current and future climate (Box 1.1). The CAIF builds on the OECD's Policy Framework for Investment (PFI) and FDI Qualities Policy Toolkit, while incorporating insights from other relevant initiatives including the High-level Approach to Enhance and Better Integrate OECD Work on Infrastructure. It does not prejudge the outcomes of international processes in relation to climate change, investment or related topics.

This chapter provides the rationale for developing the CAIF, outlines the links with OECD standards on sustainable investment, and explains how governments can use the CAIF to enhance resilience to climate change.

Box 1.1. Defining adaptation investments

This Framework adopts an inclusive definition of adaptation investments, encompassing all investments that help to build resilience to the impacts of climate change. This definition focusses on the expected impact of the investment, rather than how it is labelled or the intention behind the activities being undertaken. Building on the approach of Mullan and Ranger (2022[1]), adaptation investments should meet the following three criteria:

- **Resilience benefits**: the investment should increase resilience to climate change, by directly reducing physical climate risks or by supporting adaptation by others.
- **Do No Significant Harm**: the investment does not negatively affect the resilience of other people or ecosystems, for example by increasing the risks faced by neighbouring communities.
- **Compatible with adaptation plans**: the investment should be compatible with national or local strategies, such as National Adaptation Plans, Nationally Determined Contributions or National Disaster Reduction Strategies. If such plans do not exist, or do not set objectives in relation to the investment, the presumption is that an investment is compatible.

These criteria aim to ensure that the investment is likely to have a positive impact on adaptation and reduce the risk that the measure is ineffective or counterproductive (i.e. the risk of maladaptation).

A major challenge in defining and measuring adaptation investments is that adaptation is not a well-defined set of activities, as it depends upon the context in which the investment takes place. Addressing climate change may be only one of several motivations for undertaking an activity. For example, the activity could be an office refurbishment, with one element of this being the installation of mechanical ventilation to increase thermal comfort during hotter summers. The decision maker may not even view these components as being driven by climate adaptation but rather an effort to reduce exposure to risks or take advantage of any localised opportunities arising from a changing climate. These investments will be context specific and vary in terms of scale, and location. As such, proxies and estimation may have to be used to understand the extent to which investment flows are consistent with climate resilience objectives (Noels et al., 2024[2])

The concept of adaptation is closely linked to the concept of resilience, which is the "capacity of interconnected social, economic and ecological systems to cope with a hazardous event, trend or disturbance, responding or reorganizing in ways that maintain their essential function, identity and structure" (IPCC, 2022[3]). For the purposes of this report, climate adaptation is the process that is intended to lead to the outcome of improved resilience to the impacts of climate change.

Opportunities for investment to reduce the costs of climate impacts

Climate change is giving rise to a diverse range of increasingly severe hazards, including heatwaves, wildfires and storms (see Table 1.1). Proactive investments in adaptation – such as risk-reducing infrastructure, climate-resilient infrastructure and improved agricultural practices – can save lives, avoid losses and contribute to economic growth. Investment needs are context specific, but a growing body of literature provides an indication of the overall scale and distribution of investment needs. Plausible estimates of annual investment needs for adaptation are in the hundreds of billions of dollars per year for developing countries (UNEP, 2023[4]).

Table 1.1. Key sectors for investment in adaptation

Sector	Climate-related hazards	Examples of potential investments
Cross-sector	All	Climate analytics and forecasting
	All	Early-warning Systems
	All	Capacity building and training
Agriculture, food and fisheries	Storms, floods, drought	New crop varieties
	Heatwaves	Cooling for livestock
	Drought	Drip irrigation
Buildings	Drought, floods, heatwaves	Natural water retention solutions (e.g. green roofs)
	Heatwaves	Retrofitting for thermal comfort
	Sea-level rise, wildfires	Relocation of exposed assets
Business and industry	Floods	Property-level flood barriers
	Heatwaves	Energy efficient cooling
	All	Drones and in-field sensors, smart supply chains
Infrastructure (energy, transport, communications)	Storms, heatwaves	Distributed energy generation
	Heatwaves	Installing heat-tolerant surfaces
	All	Retrofitting, smart monitoring
Natural environment and ecosystems	Ocean acidification, increased ocean temperature	Coral reef restoration
	Sea-level rise, storms	Mangrove restoration
	All	Corridors to increase ecosystem connectivity
Water and flood management	Drought, floods	Construction of new reservoirs
	Floods, sea-level rise	Flood defences (including Nature-based Solutions)
	Drought	Replacing pipes to reduce leaks

Source: Adapted and extended from BII & FMO (2024[5])

There is a growing body of research on potential investment needs for adaptation. The UNEP Adaptation Gap 2023 report consolidated and updated sectoral estimates of adaptation needs for developing countries, arriving at a total of USD 130 - 415 billion per year until the 2030s, with a central estimate of USD 240 billion per year (equivalent to 0.6% of developing countries' GDP). The main constituents of this total were investments in flood protection, coastal protection and infrastructure, while the modelling also showed significant needs for agriculture and social protection (UNEP, 2023[4]). A separate approach, based on aggregating the needs expressed in developing countries' Nationally Determined Contributions found that the main priorities identified were for water, infrastructure and agriculture (UNFCCC, 2022[6]). There are, however, still significant evidence gaps and inherent methodological challenges (OECD, 2015[7]), which mean that these estimates should be viewed as indicative.

There are currently no comprehensive estimates of investment needs for adaptation in OECD countries, but some indications are available from national and supranational studies. For example, in France, one study identified annual investment needs by the public sector of EUR 2.3 billion per year, including measures to address overheating in buildings, improve the climate resilience of infrastructure, manage wildfires and improve water management (I4CE, 2022[8]). An analysis for the UK estimated that addressing the 61 main risks identified in the 3rd Climate Change Risk Assessment could require annual investment (both public and private) in the region of GBP 5 billion per year (EUR 5.8 billion) (Watkiss, 2022[9]).

The available quantitative evidence suggests that large investment needs are likely to arise across agriculture, infrastructure, flood management, water management and buildings. These investments include nature-based solutions. Cross-sectoral interventions to provide early warnings, improve access to climate data and build capacity are critical for managing climate risk, even if smaller in quantitative terms. Significant public and private investment will be required, but the share will vary by country context and specific investment (see chapter 2). There is very limited quantitative data on business and industry and in relation to the natural environment and ecosystems (UNEP, 2023[4]). However, given that these sectors will be sensitive to the climate and are economically significant, it is likely that they will be important for investment in adaptation. An overview of the key sectors, the potential hazards they are exposed to, and examples of potential investments are provided below in Table 1.1.

Climate change impacts are interconnected, and the actions needed to manage a risk may lie in other sectors. For example, reducing the risk of excess mortality from heat may require investments to improve the thermal performance of buildings (including hospitals) and improved infrastructure to reduce the risk of power cuts during heatwaves. Improved early warning systems can be used to put in place preventative measures before a heatwave occurs, as is used by France's heatwave plan (Agence Régionale de Santé, 2024[10]). As such, the table above focusses on the sectors where investments are expected to occur, while recognising that these will give rise to wider social and economic benefits.

These estimates of likely investment needs are significantly in excess of recorded finance flows. Climate finance provided and mobilised by developed countries for adaptation in developing countries reached USD 32.4 bn in 2022 (OECD, 2024[11]). The most comprehensive estimates currently available have identified an annual average of USD 63 billion of finance for adaptation in 2021/22, albeit with significant gaps in coverage (CPI, 2023[12]). Even allowing for underreporting of adaptation-relevant finance from some sources, there is an urgent need to scale-up investment in adaptation to become commensurate with the challenge posed by climate change.

Addressing the adaptation investment gap will require concerted efforts to mobilise finance flows from all sources – public and private, domestic and international – for increased investment in adaptation. This has been recognised by Article 2.1c of the Paris Agreement, which call for "[m]aking finance flows consistent with a pathway towards low greenhouse gas emissions and climate-resilient development". Previous OECD analysis has analysed how to scale-up climate finance as a key resource to support adaptation in developing countries (OECD, 2023[13]). For all countries, efforts are needed to strengthen the policy enabling environment for investment in adaptation (Mullan and Ranger, 2022[1]).

The need to increase investment in adaptation is taking place against a challenging macroeconomic context (OECD, 2023[14]). In many countries, high levels of public debt, high inflation and low near-term prospects for economic growth are putting pressure on public finances. Many developing countries have limited fiscal space for investments in adaptation. These broader trends are also pushing up the cost of capital, creating challenges for private investment. These trends are exacerbating the challenges to investment in adaptation (Chapter 2). In this context, this Framework is intended to support a strategic, targeted and evidence-based approach for mobilising finance from all sources for investment in adaptation. This approach reflects the common elements of good practice based on international experience, with the application of those principles being tailored to different country circumstances.

Building on OECD standards and tools for sustainable investment

The OECD has been a partner for many economies across all continents to share its expertise in reforming investment frameworks. The insights and policy lessons from decades-long efforts to improve the investment climate have been distilled into a set of tools and standards that policy makers can use to enhance the attractiveness of their economies as sustainable investment destinations (Figure 1.1).

Figure 1.1. OECD standards and tools for sustainable investment

OECD Recommendation on the Policy Framework for Investment (2015)

- ✓ Comprehensive and systematic approach for investment climate reforms. Covers 12 policy dimensions.
- ✓ Emphasises the principles of rule of law, transparency, non-discrimination and protection of property rights.

OECD Recommendation on FDI Qualities for Sustainable Investment (2022)

- ✓ Commitment to whole-of-government approach to using policy and institutions to increase sustainable FDI and deliver on the 2030 SDGs.
- ✓ First government-backed standard to help policymakers finance the SDGs and fulfill commitments made in the Paris Agreement.

Source: OECD (2015); OECD (2022)

The OECD Policy Framework for Investment (PFI) is a comprehensive and systematic tool for improving investment conditions (OECD, 2015[15]). It is neither prescriptive nor binding and provides a list of key questions to guide governments through investment climate reform. The PFI takes into consideration 12 policy areas that are widely recognised as underpinning a healthy environment for all investors, from small and medium-sized firms to multinational enterprises. The three principles that apply throughout the framework are policy coherence, transparency in policy formulation and implementation, and regular evaluation of the impact of existing and proposed policies. The PFI has been used by almost 40 countries at varying levels of economic development and across all continents, as a tool for assessing investment and business climates, and for designing reforms to improve them. In addition, the PFI serves as a reference point for investment promotion agencies, businesses, trade unions, donors as they assist recipient country partners, and non-governmental organisations in their dialogue with governments.

The more recent FDI Qualities initiative complements the PFI with insights and policy recommendations to ensure that FDI contributes to the Sustainable Development Goals (SDGs) in host economies, by creating quality jobs, enhancing innovation capacity, advancing gender equality, and supporting decarbonisation (OECD, 2022[16]). While the PFI addresses investment for green growth in broad terms, the FDI Qualities tools explicitly seek to help government shape policies and institutional arrangements to improve the contribution of FDI to climate change mitigation. Neither the PFI nor the FDI Qualities tools address the specific challenges and opportunities associated with adaptation investments.[2]

The CAIF builds on the foundation of the PFI and FDI Qualities toolkit, taking these as the foundation of an effective policy enabling environment for investment in adaptation. The CAIF applies a similar diagnostic approach, offering guiding questions to help governments identify areas that are likely to be important for mobilising adaptation investments. However, the design of the CAIF has been tailored to reflect the characteristics of climate adaptation. In particular, the scope includes public investment, given that this is critical for adaptation.

Underpinning elements for an enabling environment for investment

The PFI outlines a set of horizontal pre-requisites for creating an enabling policy environment for investments, which apply also to climate adaptation investments. These factors help maintain a predictable and transparent investment environment, engage relevant stakeholders in the policy making process and reduce the costs of doing business:

- *Fairness and trust.* High levels of trust can facilitate compliance with laws and regulations, strengthen investor confidence and reduce risk aversion. Underlying trust is the expectation that public officials respect high standards of integrity, and effectively address issues around conflict of interest, corruption and fraud. This is particularly relevant in high-risk areas like public procurement, which is a major source of finance for adaptation investments.
- *Whole-of-government and inter-agency coordination.* As with investment in general, adaptation investment is an issue requiring policy responses that do not fit neatly within any single governmental department or agency. Good government requires integrating cross-disciplinary perspectives into policy, improving coordination, and facilitating resource sharing across government institutions. In particular, coordination mechanisms are needed to ensure that centre-of-government financial and planning institutions have ownership of adaptation investment needs.
- *Transparency and engagement.* More open and inclusive policy-making processes help to ensure that policies will better match the needs and expectations of citizens and businesses. Greater participation of stakeholders in policy design and implementation leads to better targeted and more effective policies. Regular consultation of the private sector can help create shared understanding of the likely impacts of climate change, identify priority investment needs and support a discussion about how these can be financed.
- *International cooperation on standards* can complement and even reinforce domestic efforts to improve the business climate. The more standards are harmonised or mutually recognised across countries, the more easily will firms be able to invest and trade internationally. This applies also to sustainable finance taxonomies and other principles and approaches for climate adaptation alignment.

Applying the Climate Adaptation Investment Framework

The Climate Adaptation Investment Framework aims to enable a pragmatic diagnosis of the policy gaps and opportunities for increasing investment in adaptation, covering enabling environment issues such as data availability, public funding, planning processes and key regulatory issues. It is structured around six building blocks, covering the policy areas that are particularly relevant for enabling investment in climate adaptation. The value added of the CAIF is in bringing together the different policy strands that are relevant for adaptation. The aim is not to break new ground in individual policy areas but to tie them together to ensure policy coherence. It does not provide ready-made reform agendas but rather helps to improve the effectiveness of any reforms that are ultimately undertaken.

This Framework is intended to provide a non-prescriptive approach to strengthening the enabling environment. It can be used in various ways and for various purposes by different constituencies, including for self-evaluation and reform design by governments and for peer reviews in regional or multilateral discussions. Users of the Framework are invited to go through each of the building blocks and use the provided guiding questions to identify potential gaps and areas for improvement. Each building block contains an explanation of the relevance of the questions, illustrated with examples of international good practice. The building blocks also include links to resources that provide further guidance on how to address any gaps that have been identified through the guiding questions.

Integration into adaptation planning processes

National planning processes for adaptation (such as National Adaptation Plans and the development of Nationally Determined Contributions) provide a key entry-point for the use of the Climate Adaptation Investment Framework (CAIF). These processes are intended to develop a coherent policy response to understand and manage the risks from climate change, reflecting also diverse needs and circumstances (Box 1.2). The CAIF can be used as an input into the development of these processes by identifying potential gaps and facilitating discussions about potential policy responses.

Several countries have started to implement dedicated adaptation investment planning processes to complement their national adaptation planning processes. These can take different forms, but the overall aim to translate national and sectoral priorities into a pipeline of investable projects through a structured process of identifying adaptation needs, prioritising investments in climate change adaptation and developing a robust financing strategy to meet those investment needs (ADB, 2023[17]). In doing so, these processes aim to help translate planning into implementation. The CAIF identifies the elements of the enabling environment that can contribute to the successful implementation of investment planning processes, while being flexible with respect to the process being undertaken.

Box 1.2. Gender, social inclusion and climate change adaptation

Climate change will affect different groups in different ways. Vulnerability and adaptive capacity is influenced by characteristics such as level of wealth, age and gender. Those can also be factors increasing the exposure to the climate hazards and threats. In the 6th Assessment Report on Impacts, Adaptation and Vulnerability, the IPCC recognises that "within populations, the poor, women, children, the elderly and indigenous peoples have been particularly vulnerable due to a combination of factors, including the gendered division of paid and/or unpaid work (high confidence)" (IPCC, 2022[18]).

For example, FAO analysed data from 24 countries to measure the impact of climate on vulnerable rural populations. The results highlight the need to tackle inequalities, noting that "female-headed households suffer average annual income losses of 8% due to heat stress and 3% due to flooding, compared to male-headed households" (FAO, 2024[19]).

In order to address these issues, governments can address those issues by conducting gender and social inclusion analyses in relevant sectors. Integration of gender mainstreaming in public policies, and gender responsive approaches in National Adaptation Plan processes to help identify context specific gender and climate change linkages, and provided recommendations. For example, in 2019, following its NAP commitment to gender-responsive actions, Suriname developed a Water Sector Adaptation Strategy (SASAP), which includes a gender-responsive approach. This strategy has highlighted the role of women in national water governance at all levels and gender issues in the water resources sector (NAP Global Network, 2022[20])

Source: IPCC (2022[18]); FAO (2024[19]); NAP Global Network (2022[20]).

References

ADB (2023), *Climate Adaptation Investment Planning*, https://www.adb.org/publications/climate-adaptation-investment-planning-brochure. [17]

Agence Régionale de Santé (2024), *Plan canicule*, https://www.iledefrance.ars.sante.fr/mise-en-oeuvre-et-suivi-du-plan-canicule-en-ile-de-france. [10]

BII & FMO (2024), *Climate Investment Playbook*, https://assets.bii.co.uk/wp-content/uploads/2024/06/27090623/Climate-Investment-Playbook.pdf (accessed on 28 June 2024). [5]

CPI (2023), *Global Landscape of Climate Finance 2023*, Climate Policy Initiative, https://www.climatepolicyinitiative.org/wp-content/uploads/2023/11/Global-Landscape-of-Climate-Finance-2023.pdf (accessed on 29 April 2024). [12]

FAO (2024), *The unjust climate: Measuring the impact of climate change on rural, poor, women and youth*, FAO, https://doi.org/10.4060/cc9680en. [19]

I4CE (2022), "ENSURING SUFFICIENT MEANS TO ADAPT TO CLIMATE CHANGE CONSEQUENCES IN FRANCE: WHAT ARE THE COSTS?", https://www.i4ce.org/en/publication/ensuring-sufficient-adapt-climate-change-consequences-france-costs/ (accessed on 5 July 2024). [8]

IPCC (2022), *Climate Change 2022: Impacts, Adaptation and Vulnerability*, Cambridge University Press, Cambridge, UK and New York, USA. [18]

IPCC (2022), "Summary for Policymakers", in Pörtner, H. et al. (eds.), *Climate Change 2022: Impacts, Adaptation, and Vulnerability. Contribution of Working Group II to the Sixth Assessment Report of the Intergovernmental Panel on Climate Change*, Cambridge University Press, Cambridge, UK. [3]

Mullan, M. and N. Ranger (2022), "Climate-resilient finance and investment: Framing paper", *OECD Environment Working Papers*, No. 196, OECD Publishing, Paris, https://doi.org/10.1787/223ad3b9-en. [1]

NAP Global Network (2022), *Gender-responsive National Adaptation Plan (NAP) processes: Progress and promising examples*, International Institute for Sustainable Development, https://napglobalnetwork.org/resource/gender-responsive-nap-processes-progress-promising-examples/. [20]

Noels, J. et al. (2024), "Towards assessing the alignment of finance with climate resilience goals: Exploring options, methodologies, data, and metrics", *OECD*, No. 251, OECD, Paris. [2]

OECD (2024), *Climate Finance Provided and Mobilised by Developed Countries in 2013-2022*, Climate Finance and the USD 100 Billion Goal, OECD Publishing, Paris, https://doi.org/10.1787/19150727-en. [11]

OECD (2023), *OECD Economic Outlook, Volume 2023 Issue 2*, OECD Publishing, Paris, https://doi.org/10.1787/7a5f73ce-en. [14]

OECD (2023), *Scaling Up Adaptation Finance in Developing Countries: Challenges and Opportunities for International Providers*, Green Finance and Investment, OECD Publishing, Paris, https://doi.org/10.1787/b0878862-en. [13]

OECD (2022), *FDI Qualities Policy Toolkit*, OECD Publishing, Paris, https://doi.org/10.1787/7ba74100-en. [16]

OECD (2015), *Climate Change Risks and Adaptation: Linking Policy and Economics*, OECD Publishing, Paris, https://doi.org/10.1787/9789264234611-en. [7]

OECD (2015), *Policy Framework for Investment, 2015 Edition*, OECD Publishing, Paris, https://doi.org/10.1787/9789264208667-en. [15]

UNEP (2023), *Adaptation Gap Report 2023*, https://www.unep.org/resources/adaptation-gap-report-2023 (accessed on 30 April 2024). [4]

UNFCCC (2022), "Efforts of developing countries in assessing and meeting the cost of adaptation: Lessons learned and good practices Draft synthesis report by the Adaptation Committee in the context of the recognition of adaptation efforts of developing countries". [6]

Watkiss, P. (2022), *The Costs of Adaptation, and the Economic Costs and Benefits of Adaptation in the UK*, https://www.theccc.org.uk/publication/the-costs-of-adaptation-and-the-economic-costs-and-benefits-of-adaptation-in-the-uk-paul-watkiss/ (accessed on 6 August 2024). [9]

Notes

[1] Investment in this context refers to the acquisition of assets that are intended to produce goods or services, such as residential and commercial property, infrastructure, machinery and research & development (Gross Fixed Capital Formation). This definition excludes financial claims on real assets (such as equities or loans).

[2] The CAIF is part of the activities undertaken to expand the FDI Qualities Policy Toolkit under the FDI Qualities Implementation Roadmap, 2022-2027.

2 Framing investment in adaptation

This chapter explores the links between investment and climate change adaptation. It outlines how climate risks can affect investment returns, and how investments can be used to reduce physical climate risks. This chapter provides the foundation for the Framework by analysing the specific characteristics of investments in adaptation and how these characteristics relate to public and private investment.

The impacts of climate change are already being experienced, with changes in the frequency and severity of extreme events (such as heatwaves), as well as slow-onset changes (such as rising sea-levels and drought). In 2023, global average temperatures reached 1.45°C above the 1850–1900 average (WMO, 2024[1]). These impacts are projected to become more severe as the concentration of atmospheric greenhouse gasses increases. All sectors and regions will be affected, albeit with particularly severe consequences in developing countries due to their greater vulnerability. Urgent action is needed to address the source of these impacts by reducing emission of greenhouse gasses (climate mitigation), but also to increase resilience to the impacts of a changing climate (climate adaptation).

Investment has a critical role in tackling the impacts of climate change: it is critical for achieving the transition to net zero, which is the subject of complementary guidance (OECD, 2015[2]), as well as building resilience to the impacts of a changing climate. New investments will be required to address climate risks, while climate change will affect the risks and returns of current and future investments across all sectors of the economy.

This chapter provides further context for the Framework by exploring the links between investment and climate change adaptation, including the relationship with physical climate risks and the respective roles of the public and private sectors.

Investment opportunities to address physical climate risk

There is a two-way relationship between investment and physical climate risk[1]: these risks may affect the returns on investments, and investments can be used to reduce physical climate risks (OECD, 2024[3]).

The Intergovernmental Panel on Climate Change (IPCC)'s Sixth Assessment Report defines risk as the potential for adverse consequences to people or ecosystems (Figure 2.1). In the context of climate impacts, these risks (such as damage to property) arise from the interaction of hazard, vulnerability and exposure. The following definitions are adapted from (IPCC, 2022[4]):

- **Hazard**: the potential occurrence of an event or trend that may cause negative impacts. For example, a heatwave is a hazard (see Table 2.1).
- **Exposure**: the presence of people or assets in places or settings exposed to a hazard. For example, the number of people living in the area exposed to a heatwave.
- **Vulnerability**: the propensity or predisposition to be adversely affected. For example, older people can be particularly vulnerable to the impacts of heatwaves.

Climate change is leading to an increase in hazards, but the consequences of this increase in hazard depends upon exposure and vulnerability. The trends in exposure and vulnerability are the cumulative result of choices made by decision-makers in the public and private sectors. For example, provision of flood defences can reduce the vulnerability of a region to flood risk (investment helping to reduce physical climate risk). Meanwhile, coastal real estate may be increasingly exposed to flood risk due to rising sea levels (investment returns being affected by physical climate risk). Efforts to reduce exposure and vulnerability will be critical to reduce the economic and social costs of climate change.

A diverse set of actions will be required to reduce and manage physical climate risks by adapting to climate change. Potential responses include capacity building, reforms to planning or management, new or improved infrastructure, provision of information and changes in practice and behaviour (Biagini et al., 2014[5]). The appropriate actions will depend upon the context, and often a combination of actions will be required to manage a given risk.

Figure 2.1. IPCC Framework for Understanding Climate Risk

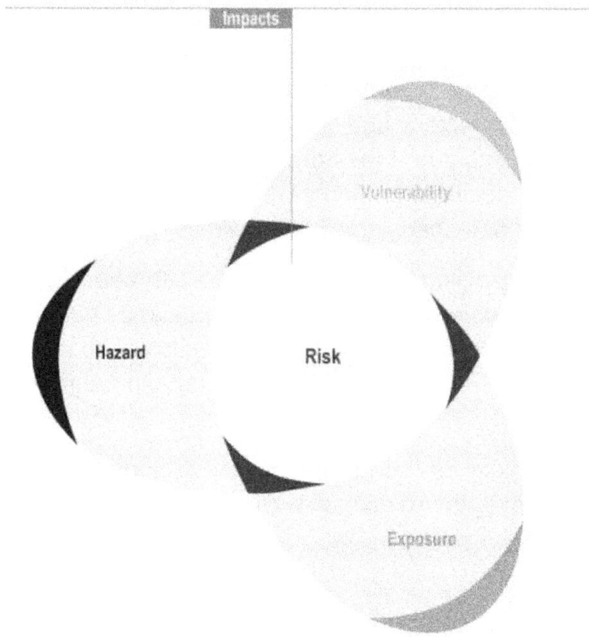

Source: IPCC AR5

Table 2.1. Examples of climate-related hazards

	Temperature-related	Wind-related	Water-related	Solid mass-related
Chronic	Changing temperature	Changing wind patterns	Changing precipitation patterns	Coastal erosion
	Heat stress		Increased hydrological variability	Soil degradation
	Temperature variability		Ocean acidification	Soil erosion
	Melting permafrost		Saline intrusion, sea-level rise, water stress	Gradual movement of soil down slopes (solifluction)
Acute	Heat wave	Cyclone, hurricanes, typhoon	Drought	Avalanche
	Frost / cold wave	Storm	Heavy precipitation	Landslide
	Wildfire	Tornado	Flood	Subsidence
			Glacial lake outburst	

Investment will be critical for implementing some of these adaptation actions. In a general sense, investment supports economic development, which helps to reduce vulnerability to climate impacts. Physical climate risk-informed investment decisions can reduce the exposure of assets to climate hazards, for example by redirecting development away from floodplains. Investment can be used to build adaptive capacity (such as training or data collection), reduce vulnerability by directly aiming to deliver adaptation actions (such as additional water storage capacity) or through the integration of adaptation actions into projects undertaken for other reasons (such as property-level flood resilience measures in a new housing development).

The desire to reduce risks and/or to realise potential opportunities provides a driver for adaptation investment. For example, farmers may change to a different crop that is more suitable for drier climates. Ski resorts may invest in facilities for summer tourism or expand access to higher altitudes in response to less reliable snowfall. Climate-related risks also create new opportunities for those supplying the goods and services that help others to address those risks through the provision of adaptation solutions, such as water-efficient industrial processes or technologies for precision agriculture that increase the efficiency of production.

Investments in adaptation can generally reduce exposure to physical climate risks, but it is neither possible nor desirable to completely eliminate these risks (OECD, 2014[6]). Managing the risk of mild flooding may be addressed by simple property-level measures, while severe flooding could require major structural changes. The degree of investment in adaptation that is motivated by a physical climate risk is therefore determined both by the characteristics of the risk, the costs and benefits of available adaptation options and the amount of residual risk that the decision-maker is willing to accept. The Sendai Framework for Disaster Risk Reduction highlights that each state has the responsibility to prevent and reduce disaster risk.

Awareness and understanding of physical climate risks

There are significant gaps in understanding physical climate risks and hence opportunities for investment in adaptation. In general, there are good data on potential climate hazards, albeit with significant gaps in coverage in developing countries. However, investors may not be fully aware of the vulnerability of their investments to climate risks (Noels et al., 2024[7]). This is particularly true of situations where climate change leads to the emergence of new risks, such as wildfires in areas that were not previously exposed, or to qualitative changes in existing risks (OECD, 2023[8]).

In addition to data gaps in the understanding of the impacts of climate hazards, there are several factors that may lead investors to underestimate their risk exposure, and hence the incentive to invest to reduce those risks:

- **Uncertainties and non-linear responses**: the climate is a complex system and projections of future climate hazards are subject to multiple sources of uncertainty, particularly at the local scale (van Bree and van der Sluijs, 2014[9]). As such, decision-makers need to consider outcomes under a range of potential scenarios, rather than just the most likely outcome.
- **Interdependencies**: climate risks may arise as a result of climate hazards occurring elsewhere, as impacts are propagated through supply chains, infrastructure networks or other sources of interdependencies.
- **Compound risks**: multiple risks materialising at the same time may have a disproportionately large impact, and – in some cases – the same climate drivers may lead to multiple hazards. For example, high temperatures and drought can lead to wildfires (Zscheischler et al., 2018[10]), and electricity blackouts as power plants have to shut down due to lack of cooling water. These blackouts then lead to the loss of mechanical cooling, thereby exacerbating the impacts on health and productivity.
- **Timing**: the impacts of a climate risk to an organisation may materialise at a different time to the occurrence of the climate hazard. For example, the economic impact of sea-level rise on a portfolio of coastal properties may occur when perceptions about risk exposure change (e.g. due to flooding elsewhere), rather than when the risk itself materialises.

In addition to potential underestimation of physical climate risks, there can be data gaps in understanding the benefits of measures to address those risks. This can lead to underestimation of the benefits of investment in adaptation and thereby make it difficult to build the business case for investment.

Distinctive characteristics of adaptation investments

Firms' behaviour will change as they start to factor in the physical evidence of climate change and this will drive investment decisions. This process is known as autonomous adaptation. For example, farmers may change the crops they grow, or building owners may install mechanical ventilation to address the consequences of hotter summers. In general, each actor will be best placed to decide on the appropriate adaptation responses for their circumstances, based on local knowledge and their own risk preferences. Changes in relative prices may encourage the conservation of scare resources, even in the absence of top-down planning.

There are, however, a set of distinctive features that apply to many investments in adaptation that mean autonomous adaptation alone is unlikely to lead to sufficient investment in adaptation (Cimato and Mullan, 2010[11]; Frontier Economics and PWA, 2022[12]):

- **Behavioural barriers, including short-termism:** the direct benefits of adaptation investments may only be fully realised as a reduction in losses when an extreme climate event occurs. Climate change is affecting the probability and severity of some events occurring now (e.g., floods, heatwaves), but it may still be several years or decades before the relevant events occur and the direct benefits of the adaptation measure become visible.
- **Distributional issues:** vulnerability to climate change is exacerbated by poverty and other forms of socio-economic disadvantage. The communities and countries with the greatest adaptation needs can also have the fewest resources to meet those needs. Public finance may have a role in supporting investment within low-income communities. At the international level, climate finance and development co-operation have a critical role in supporting adaptation in developing countries (OECD, 2022[13]; OECD, 2023[14]).
- **Strong government role:** sectors that are particularly relevant for climate adaptation also tend to be the sectors with strong existing government involvement for other reasons. These sectors include agriculture, infrastructure and provision of social services. This government role includes the provision and financing of public goods and services, as is often the case for protective infrastructure, or regulation (e.g., agriculture, environmental protection, land-use planning and building codes, price regulation of infrastructure utilities).
- **Interdependencies and coordination challenges:** the ability of an investment to enhance resilience depends upon the characteristics of the system in which it is embedded. Addressing a climate risk may require coordinated interventions across the system rather than piecemeal investments. For example, addressing drought risk may require investments on the demand side (e.g. drip irrigation) and the supply side (e.g. reducing leaks, increasing storage capacity). As such, there can be the need to address coordination challenges.
- **Externalities:** adaptation investments can yield positive or negative externalities. For example, the use of air conditioning can exacerbate the urban heat island effect, while green roofs can have positive impacts. Effective regulatory environments should limit negative externalities, but conversely it is hard to monetise the benefits of positive externalities.

These factors can distort the relationship between the perceived private return and the social return, leading to underinvestment by the private sector. They can also deter investment by increasing transaction costs. Meanwhile, public investment can be hindered by coordination challenges, insufficient recognition of climate resilience benefits in policy appraisal, and procurement policies that fail to account for the benefits of climate resilience.

Investments made autonomously may also be ineffective or counter-productive from a societal level due to market failures or policy distortions (Mullan and Ranger, 2022[15]). For example, building flood defences to protect one area can increase the risk faced by downstream locations. Measures that may make sense from a short-term perspective, such as extracting groundwater to substitute for declining rainfall, may store up larger problems for the future when groundwater supplies are exhausted. The regulatory framework will be critical to encourage effective adaptation measures and discourage or prevent measures that increase the risks faced by others. Undertaking risk-based due diligence can help businesses avoid activities that undermine resilience of communities and ecosystems.

Roles of the public sector

The public sector has a critical role in supporting adaptation investment, both through investments made directly and through the effect of public policy on the broader enabling environment for investment. For the former, critical investments relevant for climate change adaptation are often provided by governments because they are inherently difficult to fund privately. For example, governments are usually responsible for investing in protective infrastructure, even if some of that infrastructure is supplied by the private sector. Public goods, such as early warning systems and hydro-met services, are central to reducing damages from extreme events.

More generally, public investment is critical for climate adaptation because it is driven by policy objectives rather than profit maximisation. Investments are still expected to deliver a stream of benefits in return for the capital invested, but these can be wider social or economic benefits rather than a purely financial return. This is particularly relevant for adaptation, given the importance of equity as a driver for investment in adaptation, as well as the existence of non-market benefits for adaptation (such as health benefits from reduced risk of overheating). The extent to which public investment flows to adaptation depends upon the overall fiscal envelope of the public sector, the priority placed on climate adaptation and the extent to which the allocation of public funds is influenced by potential resilience benefits.

There are no comprehensive datasets covering existing domestic public finance flows for adaptation, but some initiatives have shed light on this issue. In Germany, a pilot study undertaken by UBA identified EUR 48 billion of public spending that was potentially relevant to climate change adaptation, of which EUR 1.6 – 2.5 billion was directly linked to adaptation (Haße, Hölscher and Kohli, 2024[16]). In France, an independent analysis estimated that implementing priority adaptation measures would require a budget of EUR 2.3 billion per year (I4CE, 2022[17]). A synthesis of domestic spending by developing countries found that up to 7% of domestic budgets were currently contributing to climate change adaptation (UNFCCC, 2022[18]).

International public finance has a critical role in supporting adaptation in developing countries, including through bilateral co-operation, the activities of multi-lateral development banks and dedicated climate funds. This finance source is particularly significant because the countries that are most vulnerable to climate change often lack the resources and capacity that are needed for adaptation (OECD, 2023[14]). In 2022, developed countries provided and mobilised USD 32.4 billion to support adaptation in developing countries, of which USD 29 billion was from public sources (OECD, 2024[19]). A broader approach is used by the Climate Policy Initiative, which identified a total of USD 63 billion of adaptation finance in 2021/22, of which 98% was from public sources. However, this is based on limited coverage of domestic public investment for adaptation.

Beyond public investment in adaptation, the other critical role of the public sector lies in the creation of a suitable enabling environment for private investment in adaptation. This entails ensuring that regulations and policies do not inadvertently deter investment in adaptation, for example by distorting prices or hindering the adoption of innovative approaches. It also encompasses the provision of public goods, such as climate risk maps, that can support risk-informed investment decisions. There may also be a case for providing positive incentives to support private investment that deliver wider social benefits.

The public sector's contribution to supporting investment in climate change adaptation can be constrained by a range of factors, including:

- **Fiscal constraints** – due to high levels of government debt and limitations on revenue raising, which are a particular challenge for developing countries with limited fiscal space.
- **Institutional barriers** – responsibility for climate change adaptation often lies within environment ministries, while the policy levers needed to influence public investment lie within finance and

sectoral ministries. As such, there can be a lack of capacity or coordination, particularly where investments in adaptation may cut across institutional boundaries.

- **Information gaps** – lack of data or understanding of the impact of climate-related risks, such as disruption to service delivery or contingent liabilities to public finances. Insufficient evidence or tools to consider the value of adaptation benefits to inform the allocation of public funds.

Private sector investment

Private sector investment will be a critical element of overall efforts to adapt to climate change. The private sector is a diverse category, encompassing micro-enterprises, Small and Medium Enterprises (SMEs) to large multinational corporations. Firms will have varying capacities and opportunities in relation to climate change adaptation. However, in general terms, the private sector can contribute to adaptation across three dimensions (Cochu, Hausotter and Henzler, 2019[20]):

- Investing itself in adaptation – undertaking adaptation within the boundary of the firm or in the resilience of its supply chain (e.g. retrofitting facilities to make them more resilient), ideally within the context of a broader adaptation plan.
- Providing finance for investment by others – providing the capital needed for investments that are expected to generate a market-rate return. For larger projects, this could be undertaken via project finance, while smaller projects could be funded via corporate finance (See Box 2.1).
- Providing solutions for adaptation by others – developing the goods and services that can facilitate adaptation by others (e.g. energy efficient cooling or crops suitable for a broader range of climate conditions).

Private investment across these dimensions will be primarily driven by the profit motive, and the degree of transparency, predictability, and adherence to the rule of law in a particular market. These factors provide a powerful driver to seek out opportunities, undertake innovation and deploy capital where it can earn the greatest risk-adjusted return. Effective management of climate-related risks can also serve to support long-term profitability, by reducing potential costs such as business disruption, loss of markets, legal liabilities and fines for regulatory non-compliance. Beyond the direct profit and investor confidence motives, companies may also be influenced by compliance with standards such as the OECD's Guidelines for Multinational Enterprises on Responsible Business Conduct, which call for proactive measures to adapt to climate change and avoid negative impacts on communities, workers and ecosystems (OECD, 2023[21]).

Despite the importance of private investment in adaptation, recorded private finance flows for adaptation remain very limited. Just over half (56%) of the respondents to the CDP Climate Survey 2022 identified acute physical climate risks as having a substantive impact on their business, predominantly due to concerns about losing revenues due to reduced production capacity (TCFD, 2023[22]). Climate Policy Initiative identified just USD 4.7 billion of annual private finance for adaptation between 2019 and 2022 (CPI, 2024[23])

Firms do not generally collect nor publish data on the extent to which their investments contribute to climate adaptation, nor is it readily possible to undertake a top-down analysis given that adaptation will often be embedded in investments made for other reasons. Emerging frameworks, such as the International Sustainability Standards Board (ISSB) Standards aim to provide greater transparency on private sector activity (See section 3.5). UN-led efforts on national capital accounting have made also significant strides to quantify adaptation-relevant metrics that can feed into statistical estimates of gross national product (See section 3.1). However, there is currently no systematic tracking of private finance contributing to adaptation, and reported estimates are likely to be underestimated.

Box 2.1. Project and corporate finance: implications for investment in adaptation

Private enterprises at all scales can raise capital for investment by drawing upon their existing assets (particularly their retained earnings) and/or securing external finance through borrowing or equity (shares on future profits). The mechanics for doing this will vary by scale and context: a small business may only be able to borrow from a local bank, while a larger corporation could issue bonds or issue shares.

In this process, generically known as corporate finance, the repayment of external finance is an obligation linked to the performance of the enterprise, rather than to that of a specific activity or project. The terms under which finance is available will depend upon the financial strength and credit risk of the enterprise. Corporate finance can be used to finance projects at all scales and does not have to be tied to a specific cash flow.

Project finance provides a mechanism for financing long-lived projects, where repayment is largely or entirely based on the cash-flow from the project itself, such as the sale of electricity from a renewable energy project. The benefit of this approach is that it can provide flexibility in sharing project risks. In project finance, borrowing is based on the strength of the project proposal, rather than the balance sheet of the project sponsor. However, there are higher transaction costs for project finance (e.g. legal fees, commercial advisors) which mean that its use is restricted to larger scale projects.

Corporate finance, particularly through financial intermediaries such as banks, will be critical for financing adaptation investment by SMEs and even larger firms in countries without well-developed capital markets. It will also be critical for financing worthwhile activities that do not necessarily have a direct cash flow attached, for example installing cooling to improve working conditions. Project finance is better suited to financing climate-resilient infrastructure, where there are direct revenues (such as toll roads), or under a Public-private Partnership (PPP) arrangement.

Source: Steffen (2018[24]); ADB-EBRD-IDB-IsDB-WBG (2016[25]).

Notwithstanding these reporting challenges, recorded flows of private investment in adaptation are also low due to substantive barriers to investment in adaptation. These barriers include (Tall et al., 2021[26])

- **Lack of data on climate risks**: investors may lack the underlying data required to understand the risks that they are exposed to, particularly in developing countries.
- **Low (real or perceived) returns on investment**: investors may be unable to capture the benefits of investments in adaptation due to market failures, externalities, or other market distortions. Transaction costs can be high relative to the size of the project, particularly where innovative technologies are being used, or the investment involves multiple beneficiaries.
- **Lack of strategic direction**: a lack of clear strategic direction by governments can hinder investment by increasing uncertainty (and hence perceived risk) around the future direction of government policies and investment needs. Given interdependencies, the effectiveness of a given adaptation investment will depend upon the resilience of other components of the system. A lack of clarity about the governments adaptation priorities can make it difficult for the private sector to plan.
- **Low investor confidence**: Based on existing regulatory frameworks and historic actions of governments, potential investors may have low confidence that they will encounter the transparency, predictability, and non-discriminatory enforcement of the rule of law that is required

to commit capital. Particularly in the rapidly evolving context of climate adaptation, potential investors must be provided strong evidence that they will be treated fairly, including when regulations must be modified according to the evolving situation.

Systematic efforts will be needed to address these barriers to private investment. These include the development of a supportive policy environment to overcome these barriers, while recognising the specific roles that can be played by private investment. In addition to the interventions at the policy-level, project-level interventions may also be needed to align project characteristics with the requirements of private sector participants using approaches such as blended finance for adaptation (OECD, 2024[27]).

Linking finance and funding to unlock investment

Policies will be needed to increase real economy investments in climate change adaptation. The costs of these investments can be financed from a variety (or combination) of public and private sources, via direct investment or through project finance (Figure 2.2). For these investments to occur, the characteristics of the investment need to be aligned with the requirements of potential financers and the characteristics of the finance mechanism. All finance sources expect a return commensurate with the risk and capital deployed, but the nature of this return can vary significantly (Box 2.2). For example:

- **Financial sector**: revenue stream that achieves a competitive market rate financial return, whether resulting from project finance or loans to direct investors (e.g. agri-SMEs).
- **Direct investment by corporates and SMEs**: wider variety of benefits may justify the investment, such as reduction in insurance costs, reduced risk to future profits, or potential new market opportunities.
- **Investment by the public sector**: achievement of policy goals, which could include protection of lives and livelihoods, enhancement of the natural environment.

Blended finance provides an important tool for combining public and private funding sources to achieve the desired combination of risk and return. The OECD defines blended finance as "the strategic use of development finance for the mobilisation of additional finance towards sustainable development in developing countries" (OECD, 2018[28]). Concessional public finance is used to reduce risks or improve the expected returns on a project, such that it becomes attractive to private finance. For example, certain risks can be transferred to bilateral or multilateral providers through the issuance of guarantees (Garbacz, Vilalta and Moller, 2021[29]). The OECD is currently developing a guidance on Blended Finance for Adaptation (OECD, 2024[27])).

Finance for climate-resilient investments depends on securing sufficient funding to repay the capital costs, cover ongoing operations and maintenance, and provide a return to investors. Funding sources will depend on the type of investment and broader context, but typically include public funding, user charges, land value capture and asset revenues (OECD, 2022[30]; OECD, 2024[3]). User charges can support efficiency and generate additional resources but may have adverse distributional impacts. New funding models focusing on asset recycling and land value capture can provide important sources of revenue to pay for climate resilience. These are examined in more detail in the OECD report on Infrastructure for a Climate-Resilient Future (OECD, 2024[3]).

Figure 2.2. Illustrative list of finance sources, mechanisms and adaptation investments

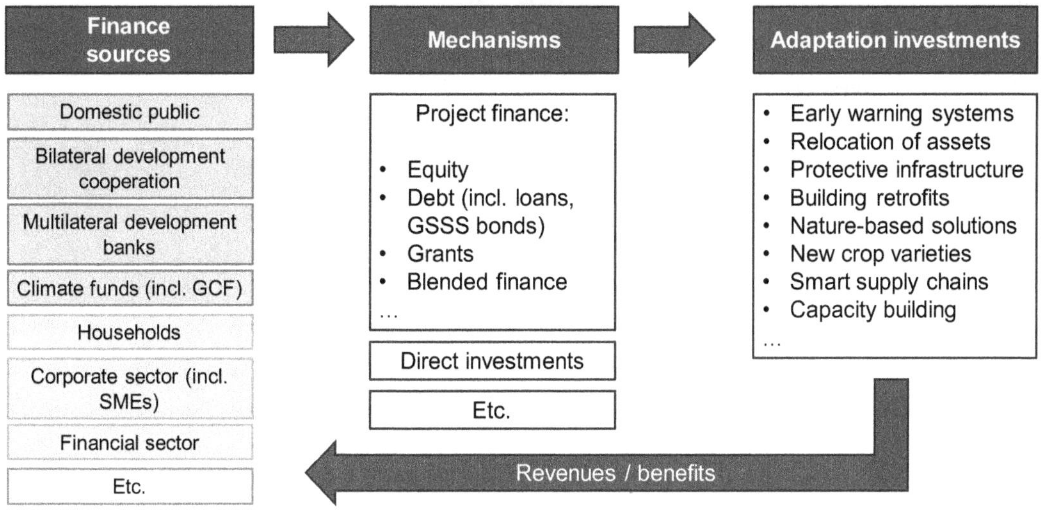

Source: Adapted from (OECD, 2023[14])

Box 2.2. Aligning project characteristics with the requirements of financing sources

The characteristics of the project need to be aligned with the requirements of different finance sources. Blended finance approaches can be used to combine different sources to ensure project viability (see (OECD, 2024[27]))

Projects with no or below market rate returns

This type of project includes those being undertaken predominantly for equity reasons (such as supporting vulnerable communities), as well as those that have the characteristics of public good (such as capacity building). Potential funding sources include:

- Domestic public finance
- Bilateral and multilateral development co-operation
- Multilateral climate funds
- Philanthropy

Projects with some revenue streams

This category covers projects that are expected to create revenues, but the expected risk and return is not commensurate with market rates. These projects could include the deployment of nature-based solutions, or the development and deployment of innovative technologies. Financing sources include:

- Development finance institutions
- National development banks
- Impact investors

Projects with market rate returns

This covers projects where the level of risk and projected returns are commensurate with market requirements. This could include climate-resilient infrastructure, such as toll roads or electricity distribution. It could also include investments to increase the efficiency of resource use, such as drip irrigation. Financing sources include:

- Banks
- Institutional investors
- Corporate investors

Source: OECD (2023[31]).

References

ADB-EBRD-IDB-IsDB-WBG (2016), *The APMG PPP Certification Guide*, https://ppp-certification.com/pppguide/download. [25]

Biagini, B. et al. (2014), "A typology of adaptation actions: A global look at climate adaptation actions financed through the Global Environment Facility", *Global Environmental Change*, Vol. 25, pp. 97-108, https://doi.org/10.1016/j.gloenvcha.2014.01.003. [5]

Cimato, F. and M. Mullan (2010), "Adapting to Climate Change: Analysing the Role of Government", *Defra Working Papers*, No. 1. [11]

Cochu, A., T. Hausotter and M. Henzler (2019), *The Roles of the Private Sector in Climate Change Adaptation – an Introduction*, Adelphi. [20]

CPI (2024), *Tracking and Mobilizing Private Sector Climate Adaptation Finance*, Climate Policy Initiative, https://www.climatepolicyinitiative.org/wp-content/uploads/2024/09/Tracking-and-Mobilizing-Private-Sector-Climate-Adaptation-Finance-2024.pdf (accessed on 3 October 2024). [23]

Frontier Economics and PWA (2022), *Barriers to financing adaptation actions in the UK*, https://www.theccc.org.uk/publication/barriers-to-financing-adaptation-actions-in-the-uk-frontier-economics-paul-watkiss-associates/ (accessed on 2 February 2023). [12]

Garbacz, W., D. Vilalta and L. Moller (2021), "The role of guarantees in blended finance", *OECD Development Co-operation Working Papers*, No. 97, OECD Publishing, Paris, https://doi.org/10.1787/730e1498-en. [29]

Haße, C., L. Hölscher and A. Kohli (2024), *Estimating Public adaptation expenditure Development and pilot application of a method in Germany*, UBA. [16]

I4CE (2022), "ENSURING SUFFICIENT MEANS TO ADAPT TO CLIMATE CHANGE CONSEQUENCES IN FRANCE: WHAT ARE THE COSTS?", https://www.i4ce.org/en/publication/ensuring-sufficient-adapt-climate-change-consequences-france-costs/ (accessed on 5 July 2024). [17]

IPCC (2022), *Climate Change 2022: Impacts, Adaptation and Vulnerability*, Cambridge University Press, Cambridge, UK and New York, USA. [4]

Mullan, M. and N. Ranger (2022), "Climate-resilient finance and investment: Framing paper", *OECD Environment Working Papers*, No. 196, OECD Publishing, Paris, https://doi.org/10.1787/223ad3b9-en. [15]

Noels, J. et al. (2024), "Towards assessing the alignment of finance with climate resilience goals: Exploring options, methodologies, data, and metrics", *OECD*, No. 251, OECD, Paris. [7]

OECD (2024), *Blended Finance for Adaptation*, OECD. [27]

OECD (2024), *Climate Finance Provided and Mobilised by Developed Countries in 2013-2022*, Climate Finance and the USD 100 Billion Goal, OECD Publishing, Paris, https://doi.org/10.1787/19150727-en. [19]

OECD (2024), *Infrastructure for a Climate-Resilient Future*, OECD Publishing, Paris, https://doi.org/10.1787/a74a45b0-en. [3]

OECD (2023), *OECD Guidelines for Multinational Enterprises on Responsible Business Conduct*, OECD Publishing, Paris, https://doi.org/10.1787/81f92357-en. [21]

OECD (2023), *Scaling Up Adaptation Finance in Developing Countries: Challenges and Opportunities for International Providers*, OECD Publishing, Paris, https://doi.org/10.1787/b0878862-en. [31]

OECD (2023), *Scaling Up Adaptation Finance in Developing Countries: Challenges and Opportunities for International Providers*, Green Finance and Investment, OECD Publishing, Paris, https://doi.org/10.1787/b0878862-en. [14]

OECD (2023), *Taming Wildfires in the Context of Climate Change*, OECD Publishing, Paris, https://doi.org/10.1787/dd00c367-en. [8]

OECD (2022), *FDI Qualities Guide for Development Co-operation: Strengthening the Role of Development Co-operation for Sustainable Investment*, OECD Development Policy Tools, OECD Publishing, Paris, https://doi.org/10.1787/7f251bac-en. [13]

OECD (2022), *G20-OECD Policy Toolkit to Mobilise Funding and Financing for Inclusive and Quality Infrastructure Investment in Regions and Cities*, https://doi.org/10.1787/99169ac9-en. [30]

OECD (2018), *Making Blended Finance Work for Sustainable Development*, https://doi.org/10.1787/9789264288768-en. [28]

OECD (2015), *Policy Guidance for Investment in Clean Energy Infrastructure: Expanding Access to Clean Energy for Green Growth and Development*, OECD Publishing, Paris, https://doi.org/10.1787/9789264212664-en. [2]

OECD (2014), *Boosting Resilience through Innovative Risk Governance*, OECD Reviews of Risk Management Policies, OECD Publishing, Paris, https://doi.org/10.1787/9789264209114-en. [6]

Steffen, B. (2018), "The importance of project finance for renewable energy projects", *Energy Economics*, Vol. 69, pp. 280-294, https://doi.org/10.1016/j.eneco.2017.11.006. [24]

Tall, A. et al. (2021), *Enabling Private Investment in Climate Adaptation and Resilience*, World Bank, Washington, DC, http://hdl.handle.net/10986/35203 (accessed on 11 April 2023). [26]

TCFD (2023), *2023 Status Report*, https://assets.bbhub.io/company/sites/60/2023/09/2023-Status-Report.pdf (accessed on 22 July 2024). [22]

UNFCCC (2022), "Efforts of developing countries in assessing and meeting the cost of adaptation: Lessons learned and good practices Draft synthesis report by the Adaptation Committee in the context of the recognition of adaptation efforts of developing countries". [18]

van Bree, L. and J. van der Sluijs (2014), "Background on Uncertainty Assessment Supporting Climate Adaptation Decision-Making", in *Adapting to an Uncertain Climate*, Springer International Publishing, Cham, https://doi.org/10.1007/978-3-319-04876-5_2. [9]

WMO (2024), *State of the Global Climate 2023*, World Meterological Organisation, https://library.wmo.int/idurl/4/68835 (accessed on 23 August 2024). [1]

Zscheischler, J. et al. (2018), "Future climate risk from compound events", *Nature Climate Change*, Vol. 8/6, pp. 469-477, https://doi.org/10.1038/s41558-018-0156-3. [10]

Notes

[1] Physical climate risks are those that result directly from the impacts of climate change (such as heatwaves or wildfires), as contrasted with transition risks which are those that may arise from the process of moving to net zero (e.g. impact of carbon pricing on carbon intensive industries).

3 The Climate Adaptation Investment Framework

This chapter provides the six "building blocks" of the Climate Adaptation Investment Framework. These collectively identify critical policies areas for enabling public and private finance to flow towards investments that support climate resilience. Each building block includes key findings, examples of international good practice, and provides diagnostic questions to identify gaps in the enabling environment. Links to further resources and guidance are provided for each building block.

The CAIF consists of six components ("building blocks") that collectively identify the policies that can enable public and private finance to flow to investments that support climate resilience. The Framework targets actions that can be led by national governments and is intended to be applied in a flexible, non-binding and non-prescriptive manner, recognising that the appropriate responses will be context specific. In this evolving policy area, the CAIF provides a baseline of good practices that draw on existing tools and resources, while identifying areas in which information gaps remain.

This Framework covers domestic policy measures, while recognising that the enabling environment for investment is influenced by a broader range of factors, including capacity and access to financial resources. It is intended to complement existing initiatives to build capacity and enhance developing countries' access to climate finance.

Each component of the CAIF outlines the key policy areas that governments should consider in trying to mobilise investment for climate adaptation, offers examples of good practice, and provides a set of diagnostic questions to guide governments in identifying priority actions (Table 3.1). These components are interlinked and intended to be mutually supportive. For example, effective strategic planning can identify priority investment needs, support for private investments can translate that concept into a viable project provided that there are suitable funding mechanisms in place. Sustainable finance tools could facilitate access to credit on more attractive terms than would otherwise be the case.

Table 3.1. Components of CAIF and guiding questions for policymakers

Component	Guiding Questions
Strategic planning and policy coherence	• Are there clear objectives for adaptation at the national level, for example through a National Adaptation Plan or Strategy? • Has adaptation been integrated into the strategies and plans for investment in key sectors (such as agriculture, infrastructure and water)? • Is there a process in place to identify adaptation investment needs and link those needs with finance sources? • Are responsibilities for managing climate-related risks clearly identified? • Are mechanisms in place to ensure that centre-of-government financial and planning institutions have ownership of adaptation and resilience investment needs? • Is there a process in place to ensure multi-stakeholder coordination and dialogue across relevant ministries, national and local agencies and the private sector on adaptation priorities and investment plans? • Is authoritative data on climate risks publicly available? For example, through a platform or data repository. • Have the potential economic risks of climate change been assessed? • Are any data collection efforts in place to monitor trends in public and private investment relevant to adaptation?
Regulatory alignment	*Sectoral* • Do agricultural support mechanisms favour specific commodities? Are payments linked to compliance with environmental regulations? • Does the regulatory system encourage resilient retrofitting of buildings? For example, is adaptation mainstreamed into existing retrofitting programmes, and do planning requirements support adaptation? • Do regulatory arrangements for business and industry facilitate investment in adaptation? For example, are climate-related risks addressed within existing health and safety legislation. • Are climate-related risks clearly identified and managed for infrastructure networks? • Do policies for economic regulation of infrastructure providers provide incentives for mainstreaming climate resilience? To what extent are investments in climate resilience viewed as allowable investments? • Are there mechanisms (such as payments for ecosystem services) in place to put a value on the services provided by the natural environment and ecosystems? • Is there an effective system in place for managing water resources, including mechanisms for reflecting the value of water? *Cross-cutting* • Are fundamental elements of investment policy in place to promote confidence in transparency and predictability, and non-discriminatory contract enforcement and dispute settlement? • Are there efforts underway to identify whether technical codes need to be updated in light of climate change? What support is available to help enable and prioritise these interventions? • Does land use planning account for the evolution of climate risks over time? Are these planning processes enforced?

Insurance and risk transfer	• Do mechanisms exist to help insurers accurately reflect climate risk? What frameworks or standard-setting tools exist to ensure the quality and accuracy of climate-risk assessments across the insurance sector? • Do mechanisms exist to motivate insurers and other institutional investors to align investments with adaptation and resilience needs? Are there clear incentives for risk reduction and resilience building activities? • Do governments help to communicate climate risks that cannot be reduced? Are risk-sharing arrangements well-understood among households, businesses, and governments at all levels? • Does the insurance market offer policies that include resilient recovery from extreme events? Are there market or regulatory barriers to such products? • Do mechanisms exist to understand the impacts of climate-related disasters on public finances? How do governments account for the costs associated with climate risk, including the ex-ante fiscal costs posed by contingent liabilities?
Public finance and investment	• Does the process of allocating budgets consider the potential impacts of climate change? • Do project or programme appraisal tools account for the benefits of adaptation? • Do public procurement policies account for benefits over the lifecycle of the investment? Do the systems for asset management aim to optimise costs of existing assets over their lifespans? • Does the process for allocating risks within PPPs account for climate risks? • Is there a strategy in place to manage the financial consequences to the public sector of climate extremes?
Sustainable finance	• Are there voluntary or mandatory standards/mechanisms or principles for identifying adaptation investments that have been adopted by market participants? How is compliance with those standards/mechanisms or principles measured and verified? • Are mechanisms in place to provide transparency about the exposure of financial assets to physical climate risks? What guidance exists to support disclosure in relation to the choice of metrics, scenarios and assumptions? • Do requirements for corporate disclosure, including transition plans, address adaptation? Do these reflect the benefits of adaptation, as well as exposure to physical climate risks? • Is there a taxonomy for green and sustainable finance? If so, does this taxonomy include criteria for climate resilience? • Is there any technical or financial support available for potential issuers of climate resilience financial instruments?
Support and incentives for private investment	• Are existing incentives to stimulate private investment in support of adaptation well-targeted and time-limited? Are measures in place to assess their cost-effectiveness? • What resources are available to help project developers understand the climate-related risks that they face and potential adaptation measures? • What support is available to help with early-stage project development? Is climate resilience systematically considered within existing mechanisms for supporting project preparation? • Are there support mechanisms in place to assist with access to climate finance, such as national climate funds? • To what extent is the existing intellectual property framework conducive to promoting investment in adaptation innovation and transfer of adaptation technologies among firms? • What support is available for early-stage innovation in adaptation? Are knowledge transfer facilities in place (e.g. technology centres, business incubators, applied research centres) to provide knowledge exchange and innovation services for adaptation technologies?

Strategic planning and policy coherence

The physical impacts of climate change will be far-reaching and systemic. Institutional coordination to develop coherent multi-sector strategies and plans can facilitate adaptation investment by creating a shared understanding of the likely impacts of climate change, identifying priority investment needs and supporting a discussion about how these can be financed. Access to climate and socio-economic data to identify and monitor evolving vulnerabilities and risks is needed to support the strategic planning process.

Institutional coordination

Climate change adaptation is a systemic challenge, both in terms of the propagation of climate risks and the development of adaptation responses. Climate impacts occurring in one area can have knock-on impacts elsewhere: for example, the flooding of a port could disrupt supply chains across the economy. Similarly, the effectiveness of a given adaptation investment will often depend upon what other measures are being undertaken. For example, the expected value of having a generator as backup will depend upon the measures that are underway elsewhere in the economy to enhance the resilience of the electricity supply.

Multiple institutions are involved in designing and implementing strategies and policies that affect investment in adaptation (see Box 3.1 for examples of national approaches). Mechanisms such as central coordination or decision-making bodies can support a comprehensive and coherent approach to adaptation planning. These mechanisms can enhance alignment and communication across ministries, sector entities, national and local agencies, and the private sector. For example, Colombia has established a national system for climate change (known as "SISCLIMA") that oversees adaptation planning. This is led by the Department of National Planning (DNP) and includes the ministers for the key sectoral ministries. Leadership by DNP helps to ensure consistency with the country's development plans (OECD, 2014[1]). In the absence of such arrangements, overlapping and sometimes conflicting rules, procedures and regulations across ministries and levels of government, including between the central and provincial levels can create administrative burdens on investors. An inclusive process is needed to engage these actors in identifying and implementing the measures needed to unlock investment.

Climate adaptation is generally the responsibility of environment ministries, yet the policy tools needed to unlock investment flows sit with other ministries and institutions responsible for financial planning and budget management, which may lack capacity and expertise in relation to climate change (CFMCA, 2022[2]). Under the Helsinki Principles, the Coalition of Finance Ministers for Climate Action developed a guide that provides a framework of options for mainstreaming climate adaptation and mitigation into the core functions, capabilities and priorities of ministries of finance (CFMCA, 2023[3]). The framework provides guidance on strengthening inter-ministerial coordination on climate change, including establishing coordination bodies and adapting the mandate of ministries of finance to include climate action. High-level councils set up through the Prime Minister that include representatives from relevant public agencies can help bridge political interests and administrative boundaries, and ensure that centre-of-government financial and planning institutions have better ownership of adaptation and resilience investment needs.

The location-specific nature of climate impacts means that effective governance of adaptation investment relies more heavily on multi-level approaches than other types of investment. National policy alignment instruments can help promote coherence in the activities of different subnational jurisdictions and ensure coordination across different levels of government and line ministries (OECD, 2023[4]). Examples relevant for adaptation include national and regional climate change councils, national adaptation policies, plans and strategies that clearly address the local level, and national urban policies with a focus on climate adaptation. Such instruments can help clarify the decision-making roles and responsibilities of national, subnational and local governments, and help identify concrete measures to be taken at different levels to ensure an enabling environment for adaptation investments.

Involvement of non-governmental actors in multi-level climate governance is useful to ensure awareness and consideration of different perspectives and increasing buy-in and support for implementation. Moreover, stakeholder engagement can play a critical role in ensuring that adaptation commitments, targets, and actions are credible and effective, and grounded in science and legitimate expertise. Experts' engagement can also come from a wide variety of stakeholders, including indigenous communities, workers and consumer groups. Inclusive processes of engagement with stakeholders are crucial to better understanding potential interdependencies between climate impacts and human rights and can provide valuable insights on how to enhance effectiveness of adaptation investments (OECD, 2023[5]). In France the High Council on Climate was established in 2018 to increase coordination between public agencies, engage relevant stakeholders and advise to the French government on the delivery of policy measures aimed at mitigating and adapting to climate change. The Council's members include climate scientists, agricultural engineers, and energy and environmental experts.

Strategic planning

Strategic planning has a critical role in supporting investment by raising awareness of climate risks and adaptation opportunities, facilitating discussion about acceptable levels of risk and identifying priority actions and policy tools to accelerate adaptation finance (OECD, 2015[6]). Planning processes can also contribute to improved institutional coordination and provide clarity about the responsibility for managing climate-related risks. National Adaptation Plans (NAPs) and Strategies provide a mechanism for doing so. Currently, all OECD countries have a plan or strategy in place. By September 2023, 143 developing countries were in the process of developing NAPs, with 49 of those countries having submitted completed documents to the UNFCCC (UNFCCC LEG, 2023[7]). However, in general, these plans and strategies have limited coverage of how the measures within the NAP or NAS will be funded, and limited discussion of how to strengthen the enabling environment for investments in adaptation. Furthermore, NAPs are often led by ministries of environment with varying degrees of government ownership. Systematic engagement of ministries of finance in NAP preparation committees can help ensure that NAPs are integrated into wider budget management processes (CFMCA, 2023[3]).

New initiatives are underway to support countries in developing the investment components of their adaptation plans and strategies, reflecting different country contexts. These include the Asian Development Bank's Climate Adaptation Investment Planning (CAIP) process, which aims to translate national adaptation plans into adaptation investment plans, which are then embedded within countries' economic and fiscal frameworks (Box 3.1). The GCF and NDC Partnership are developing a Climate Investment Planning and Mobilization Framework, which sets out a process for translating strategies into tangible investments, covering both adaptation and mitigation (GCF/NDC, 2023[8]). The UN has launched an Adaptation Pipeline Accelerator initiative, which aims to foster high-level collaborations to facilitate the translation of adaptation plans into a pipeline of bankable projects (UNDP, 2023[9]). At the national level, the Netherlands Delta Programme has identified almost EUR 31 billion of investment needed in flood defences between 2024 and 2050 (Box 3.1). Based on these and other examples, the CAIF identifies common elements of good practice, the types of policies and institutions that can play key roles, and the broader ecosystem of actors to draw upon and engage.

The development of a strategic approach to investment in adaptation should be aligned with the development of strategies for managing the financial consequences of extreme events. There are close links between strategic planning for investment in adaptation and the implementation of strategies for disaster risk financing (OECD, 2020[10]). Investments relevant to climate adaptation may be made under the heading of disaster risk management, for example. Meanwhile, the choice of risk transfer tools (such as insurance) will affect the allocation of risk and, therefore, the incentive to invest in activities to manage those risks.

Monitoring and access to data

Climate change risk is a driver of investment in adaptation (see Chapter 2), so it is essential to ensure that decision-making is informed by high-quality and reliable estimates of future climate risks. Estimates of overall climate trends are commonly available through national and regional climate centres, and initiatives such as the Global Climate Observing System (GCOS), the Group on Earth Observation (GEO) and the Copernicus Climate Change Service (C3S). International coordination serves as an important basis for the exchange and effective use of climate information for adaptation planning and implementation (UNFCCC, 2022[11]). The use of online platforms, such as Germany's KLiVO portal, can help to disseminate authoritative projections and tools to potential end users (Cabinet of Germany, 2024[12]). The World Bank Climate Change Knowledge Portal provides access to global datasets and tools, as well as climate risk country profiles for developing countries (World Bank, 2024[13]).

There is a growing number of commercial providers that offer climate risk modelling services, which aim to translate climate projections into estimates for how specific properties or businesses will be affected by climate risks (such as wildfires and floods). The working of these models tends to be proprietary and the use of different models can yield sharply different results (Roston et al., 2024[14]) (Hain, Kölbel and Leippold, 2022[15]). Governments can support the development of better quality climate-risk data through: supporting open access to relevant public data, developing guidelines for measuring the accuracy of climate models and fund foundational research (such as modelling techniques) on climate risk modelling (PCAST, 2023[16]).

In addition to better understanding climate risks, there are opportunities to use innovative approaches to identify potential opportunities for investments in climate change adaptation. For example, the Nature-based Solutions Opportunity Scan uses satellite imagery to identify potential opportunities for using NBS in coastal and urban areas (World Bank, 2024[17]). Infrastructure systems models have been developed to understand how climate change will affect infrastructure networks and the benefits of investing in resilience measures, for example in the case of Ghana (Adshead et al., 2022[18]). National statistical bodies and international organisations can support these efforts by developing natural capital accounting systems with adaptation-relevant metrics. For example, the United States is currently developing a system to monetise natural assets that could be used to better understand the benefits of preserving and investing in ecosystems that help reduce the damages of climate change (Box 3.1).

It will also be important to ensure that mechanisms are in place to monitor investment flows relevant to climate change adaptation, and especially relating to the mobilisation of private finance in this context (OECD, 2024[19]). This can increase transparency, support international assessments of progress and inform the development and revision of subsequent cycles of strategic approaches. Expansion of the FDI Qualities Indicators to cover adaptation investment will provide a better understanding of the relative contributions of public, private domestic and cross-border investment to adaptation. Developing reliable indicators will however depend on improving the availability of reliable, timely and internationally comparable information on adaptation investment flows. There is currently good coverage of international public finance flows, while there is limited coverage of private finance flows and domestic public finance flows (OECD, 2023[20]). Ongoing work in the OECD is exploring options for measuring the alignment of finance flows with adaptation and resilience goals. Options for filling these gaps are discussed in the following components: public finance and investment and sustainable finance.

Guiding questions

- Are there clear objectives for adaptation at the national level, for example through a National Adaptation Plan or Strategy?
- Has adaptation been integrated into the strategies and plans for investment in key sectors (such as agriculture, infrastructure and water)?
- Is there a process in place to identify adaptation investment needs and link those needs with finance sources?
- Are responsibilities for managing climate-related risks clearly identified?
- Are mechanisms in place to ensure that centre-of-government financial and planning institutions have ownership of adaptation and resilience investment needs?
- Is there a process in place to ensure multi-stakeholder coordination and dialogue across relevant ministries, national and local agencies and the private sector on adaptation priorities and investment plans?
- Is authoritative data on climate risks publicly available? For example, through a platform or data repository.
- Have the potential economic risks of climate change been assessed?
- Are any data collection efforts in place to monitor trends in public and private investment relevant to adaptation?

Relevant tools and resources

Topic	Resource
Strategic planning	European Commission – Guidelines on Member States' adaptation plans and strategies OECD – Recommendation on Disaster Risk Financing Strategies World Bank – Adaptation Principles: A guide for designing strategies for climate change adaptation and resilience UNFCCC LEG – Technical guidelines for the NAP process UNDRR – Guide for adaptation and resilience finance
Institutional coordination and private sector engagement	Asian Development Bank – Accelerating Private Sector Engagement in Adaptation in Asia and the Pacific CFMCA – A Framework and Guide for Ministers and Ministries of Finance GIZ – Multi-level climate governance supporting local action NAP GN – Toolkit for Engaging the Private Sector in National Adaptation Plans (NAPs) OECD – Blended Finance for Adaptation - *forthcoming* OECD – Climate adaptation: Why Local Governments cannot do it alone OECD – Lessons on Engaging with the Private Sector to Strengthen Climate Resilience OECD – FDI Qualities Policy Toolkit OECD – Infrastructure for a Climate-Resilient Future World Bank and UNDRR – Enabling Private Investment in Climate Adaptation & Resilience
Monitoring and access to data	OECD – International Programme for Action on Climate dashboard OECD – Measuring Progress in Adapting to a Changing Climate UN-OECD – Coalition of national statistical bodies UNFCCC – Methodologies for assessing adaptation needs and their application World Bank – Climate Change Knowledge Portal WMO – Guide to Climatological Practices WRI – Overview of 100+ Climate Data platforms

Box 3.1. Case studies: strategic planning and policy coherence

Asian Development Bank's Climate Adaptation Investment Planning process

The Asian Development Bank is working with 12 countries in the Asia-Pacific region to support them in translating their adaptation priorities in key sector(s), as set out in NAPs or NDCs, into Adaptation Investment Plans. These plans are intended to be embedded in the countries' medium-term planning and fiscal frameworks. It follows a structured process that aims to diagnose the overall enabling environment, understand adaptation needs, prioritise investments and identify appropriate financing opportunities. It is designed to integrate with each country's system for public financial management to ensure that adaptation needs are integrated into overall fiscal decisions. The process brings together finance ministries, sectoral ministries and the ministry responsible for climate change.

Netherlands' Delta Programme

Water management is a high priority in the Netherlands given that around 26% of the country lies below sea-level and around 60% of the country is susceptible to flooding. The 2012 Delta Act created the current structure for planning to manage flood risks, aiming to support a coherent and adaptive approach in the face of pressures including climate change. Planning takes a consensus-based approach bringing together relevant ministries, local authorities and water boards and is led by the Delta Commissioner. Each year, a Delta Programme is published featuring specific investments and suggested policy measures. Implementation of specific investments is largely funded through a Delta Fund (a dedicated element within the national budget), which includes a total budget of EUR 25 billion for measures between 2024-2037. This planning process takes a long-term perspective (until 2050) and sets out tangible objectives, aligned with secure long-term funding.

UK Climate Change Committee and Adaptation Committee

The UK Climate Change Committee (CCC) is an advisory body designed to provide feedback and evaluation of government progress on climate action. With respect to adaptation, the CCC is required by statute to monitor, evaluate, and report on progress and advise policymakers on the risks and opportunities presented by climate change. In 2009, the CCC established the Adaptation Committee, which develops biennial adaptation progress reports of the UK's NAP, Scotland's Climate Change Adaptation Program and an independent climate change risk assessment. As an independent statutory body with considerable leadership across the UK governments, the CCC model helps to ensure strategic alignment, policy coherence, and accountability, and has been emulated by other countries around the world as a result.

Natural Capital Accounting in the United States

The US National Strategy to Develop Statistics for Environmental-Economic Decisions, launched in 2023, creates a system to monetise natural capital, providing metrics to help monitor changes in the condition and economic value of land, water, air and other natural assets. Such a Natural Capital Accounting (NCA) system can help mainstream climate adaptation in policy making and improve understanding of both climate risks and the benefits of investing in adaptation. For example, NCA metrics can be used to record and model climate change outcomes on ecosystems, or to estimate the economic value of preserving natural defences against climate-related disasters (e.g. reefs, dunes, forests reduce the damage cause by storms and floods).

Source: ADB (2023[21]); Delta Programme (2023[22]); van Buren (2019[23]); OECD (2024[24]); White House (White House, 2023[25]).

Regulatory alignment to reflect the benefits of climate resilience

Aligning regulatory arrangements and resolving market failures can strengthen the incentive to invest in activities that enhance climate resilience, while discouraging investments that undermine resilience to climate change. This building block identifies critical issues in key sectors for adaptation: agriculture, buildings, business and industry, infrastructure, natural environment and ecosystems, and water. It also identifies transversal areas including technical codes and standards.

A fair, transparent, clear and predictable regulatory framework for investment is a critical determinant of investment decisions and their contribution to development priorities, including climate adaptation (OECD, 2015[26]). Taking measures to enhance the quality of the regulatory framework and its effective implementation is particularly important for investors to navigate the complex policy space around climate adaptation (see Chapter 1).

Autonomous adaptation will be a critical driver of adaptation investment, but sectors that are critical for climate change adaptation often have high levels of government intervention for reasons unrelated to climate (Cimato and Mullan, 2010[27]). Regulatory frameworks that were implemented for reasons unrelated to climate change can nonetheless hinder desired investment, by distorting prices or creating regulatory hurdles to adaptation investment. Examples of efforts to achieve this are provided in Box 3.3.

Regulatory alignment is also critical for ensuring that investments made by businesses to manage their own exposure to the physical risks of climate change do not lead to increases in the risks faced by third parties, such as suppliers or neighbouring communities. The OECD standard for Responsible Business Conduct call on business to "avoid activities which undermine climate adaptation for, and resilience of, communities, workers and ecosystems" (OECD, 2023[5]). For example, this can mean ensuring that cooling infrastructure is available to avoid exposing workers to unacceptable levels of heat. Regulatory alignment can support this goal by discouraging behaviour that negatively affects third parties.

Addressing regulatory misalignments in key sectors

The regulatory environment is particularly critical for sectors that are heavily exposed to the impacts of climate change, and already subject to considerable government intervention. Critical sectors will vary by country, but this section focusses on key aspects of the regulatory regime in sectors that will frequently be important for investment in adaptation (see Chapter 1).

The *agricultural* sector will be critical for investment in adaptation, as farmers seek to adjust their practices in the face of climate change impacts on this climate-sensitive sector. There are high levels of government intervention in this sector globally, with an annual average of USD 851 billion of support to agriculture in 2020-22, including USD 630 billion of direct support to producers[1] (OECD, 2023[28]). Market price support measures (such as import tariffs, minimum prices and export taxes) may potentially hinder adaptation to climate conditions. Direct payments for individual agricultural commodities may also slow down the necessary re-adjustments in production patterns to prepare the sector for changing climate; the annual average payments in 2020-22 amounted to USD 380 billion (OECD, 2023[28]). Input subsidies can contribute to the inefficient use of water, fertiliser and energy. Reducing and redirecting distorting forms of agricultural support can increase the incentive to adapt, while also potentially improving public finances. There is also the potential for agricultural policy to provide positive support for investment in adaptation, by considering climate change impacts and necessary measures on the sector, detailing them as a plan for each field and crop (see Box 3.3 for the example of Japan's agricultural adaptation plan).

Regulations covering *business and industry* may need to be examined to ensure that they are conducive to managing climate risk, and hence encourage investment in climate change adaptation. In particular, these regulations can help to ensure that efforts by businesses to manage their physical climate risk do not increase the risks faced by others. Some key areas include:

- Health and safety requirements: climate change may have a negative impact on worker health and safety, for example through increasing the risk of overheating for those working outside. Regulations covering worker health and safety may need to be updated to account for new risks, or changes in the characteristics of current risks.
- Business continuity planning: regulations can be used to encourage businesses that provide critical services to better understand and plan for climate-related risks, as part of broader business continuity planning.
- Responsible business conduct: the OECD Guidelines for Multinational Enterprises on Responsible Business Conduct provide a benchmark for ensuring that adaptation measures do not have negative impacts on ecosystems or communities (see Box 3.2).

Buildings are vulnerable to the impacts of climate change (e.g. damage from subsidence or wildfires) and also influence the vulnerability of their inhabitants to climate risks (such as health impacts from overheating). Land use planning and technical codes (discussed below) are critical for influencing new buildings and major renovations, but further measures may also be required to support investment in retrofitting of the existing building stock. These include:

- Examine planning and zoning policies that may hinder retrofitting measures, such as external shading or installing light-coloured roofs.
- Integrate climate change adaptation with energy efficiency retrofitting programmes to reduce costs and avoid inadvertent tensions.
- Support transparency about the climate resilience of buildings, for example through voluntary labelling initiatives.
- Encourage retrofitting of rental properties through support measures (such as retrofitting subsidies) or regulatory requirements, particularly with regard to the provision of social housing.

Infrastructure regulation is a critical element for unlocking investment in climate-resilient communications, energy and transport networks. The contribution of economic regulation and standards are discussed below. In addition to these, critical areas for examining regulation include (OECD, 2024[29]).:

- Implementing requirements for securely sharing information between infrastructure sectors, given that climate-related risks can propagate through infrastructure networks.
- Using proportionate regulatory requirements (such as financial penalties for service disruption) to encourage infrastructure operators to internalise climate-related risks therefore invest to manage those risks.
- Ensuring a clear allocation of climate-related risks throughout the infrastructure lifecycle.
- Examining permitting and environmental impact assessment processes to ensure that they are conducive to investment in climate-resilient infrastructure.

Box 3.2. Responsible Business Conduct and investment in climate change adaptation

The OECD Guidelines for Multinational Enterprises (MNEs) on Responsible Business Conduct provide recommendations from governments to MNEs about how they can contribute to sustainable development while avoiding adverse consequences from their activities. The Guidelines cover a breadth of themes including human rights, labour rights, environment and anti-bribery. They have been endorsed by 51 jurisdictions that account for two thirds of global trade, and serve as an internationally recognised source of good practice. Although the Guidelines are voluntary, the underlying principles may be embedded within domestic legislation or international agreements. The implementation of the Guidelines is supported by a network of National Contact Points, which provide a non-judicial grievance mechanism if enterprises are not in compliance with the guidelines.

The Guidelines provide a mechanism for supporting investment in adaptation by encouraging enterprises to manage their exposure to the risks of climate change in ways that also support the resilience of the communities in which they operate. RBC principles and standards, including risk-based due diligence, call on business to implement adaptation measures as needed and "avoid activities which undermine climate adaptation for, and resilience of, communities, workers and ecosystems".

Source: OECD (2023[5])

Natural environment and ecosystems underpin economic activity and well-being, yet these are under severe pressure due to human activity. Climate change is putting further pressure on ecosystems and is driving biodiversity loss (IPCC, 2022[30]). An underlying challenge is that the benefits of ecosystems are frequently not valued by markets, leading to unsustainable practices and underinvestment in preserving natural capital. Regulation, economic instruments and information can all play a role in encouraging investment in adaptation in this sector (OECD, 2021[31]): putting a price on the use of natural resources, through taxes or charges, can discourage harmful investments (such as conversion of forest). The use of positive incentives, such as payments for ecosystem services, can provide an additional revenue stream for adaptation investments in this sector, such as the use of Nature-based Solutions.

The *water* cycle will be a significant transmission mechanism for the impacts of climate change, with negative impacts on the reliability of water supply and water quality. Regulations guiding the use of water will therefore shape adaptation responses. A key structural challenge is that the prices of water faced by some end-users, such as agriculture or industry, does not necessarily reflect its value (GCEW, 2023[32]). A related issue is that systems for water allocation that were designed under the assumption of a static climate are no longer fit-for-purpose in a changing climate (OECD, 2013[33]). The OECD's Recommendation on Water identifies a number of good practices (OECD, 2016[34]):

- Manage water at the appropriate scale(s) within integrated basin governance systems to reflect local conditions, and foster co-ordination between the different scales.
- Implement water demand management policies that build on an understanding of ecological limits and are informed by short- and longer-term projections and account for uncertainties on current and future water availability and demand.
- Consider using economic instruments for water resources management (e.g. water abstraction charges), support for water-efficient technologies or for the use of alternative sources of water (e.g. reclaimed water).

The implementation of these good practices for realising the value of water will often require a coherent package of reform measures to ensure that the required data are available, suitable governance mechanisms are in place and regulatory arrangements are aligned to national circumstances. For example, the Climate Resilient Water Sector in Grenada project includes governance and regulatory reforms, combined with support for end-users to reduce their consumption (see Box 3.3). The OECD also supports governments in improving their systems for water management through a series of Regional and National Policy Dialogues on water (OECD, 2024[35]).

Updating regulations and standards across all sectors

Technical codes and other regulatory standards often need to be updated to account for the impacts of climate change (Cançado and Mullan, 2020[36]). For example, road surface specifications may need to be updated to account for higher summer temperatures. These can also act as a barrier to the adoption of innovative technologies, where technical codes presuppose the use of a particular technology, such as requiring a certain capacity for drainage when it may be better to let the water percolate into the soil. Canada is investing to update its national technical codes through the Climate Resilient Built Environment Initiative and the Standards to Support Resilience in Infrastructure initiative (see Box 3.3). These initiatives aim to support the updating of national codes, and providing the underlying evidence needed to demonstrate the performance of innovative adaptation solutions. The use of performance-based standards can help to unlock the potential for innovative approaches, because they target outcomes rather than mandating specific approaches.

Land use planning is also a critical area for directing investment towards areas that are less exposed to climate hazards. As well as preventing inappropriate development in highly exposed areas, effective land-use planning arrangements provide a signal to investors about the relative riskiness of various locations, thereby helping to avoid the accumulation of exposure to physical climate risk. To be effective, land use planning should be informed by climate data to understand how climate hazards may evolve, be developed in an inclusive manner and effectively enforced. For example, the Green Climate Fund is supporting modelling of areas that are highly exposed to climate risks to inform the update of Tunisia's Master Land-use Plan (GCF, 2021[37]) The alignment of incentives between layers of government can also be relevant, for example if the benefits of developments accrue at the local level, while the costs of disaster response and reconstruction are picked up at the state or national level.

Economic regulation of infrastructure networks

Infrastructure networks are often natural monopolies, meaning that it is not feasible for them to be provided competitively. For example, electricity transmission and distribution, railway networks and water supply and sanitation are usually provided by a single supplier in a specific area. Given the absence of competition, prices and requirements for service quality are often determined by an economic regulator. The objectives of regulators will vary, but in general terms the aim is to ensure a balance between affordability and service quality, while allowing private owners to earn a reasonable rate of return on the capital invested.

The structure of economic regulation has a key impact on the willingness and capacity of the regulated firm to invest in climate change adaptation. The following elements of the regulatory structure can influence investment in adaptation (OECD, 2024[29]):

- Allowable investments: ensuring that decision on whether to allow investments by the regulated utility account for the benefits of resilience.
- Performance standards: adjusting performance standards to reflect changing risks from climate change, covering both risks to service provision (such as supply disruption) and risks from service provision (such as the failure of dams during heavy rainfall).
- Additional requirements: regulators can raise awareness of climate risks through requirements to undertake stress tests, identify interdependencies and report on adaptation plans

Guiding questions

Sectoral

- Do *agricultural* support mechanisms favour specific commodities? Are payments linked to compliance with environmental regulations?
- Does the regulatory system encourage resilient retrofitting of *buildings*? For example, is adaptation mainstreamed into existing retrofitting programmes, and do planning requirements support adaptation?
- Do regulatory arrangements for *business and industry* facilitate investment in adaptation? For example, are climate-related risks addressed within existing health and safety legislation.
- Are climate-related risks clearly identified and managed for *infrastructure* networks?
- Do policies for economic regulation of infrastructure providers provide incentives for mainstreaming climate resilience? To what extent are investments in climate resilience viewed as allowable investments?
- Are there mechanisms (such as payments for ecosystem services) in place to put a value on the services provided by the *natural environment and ecosystems*?
- Is there an effective system in place for managing *water* resources, including mechanisms for reflecting the value of water?

Cross-cutting

- Are fundamental elements of investment policy in place to promote confidence in transparency and predictability, and non-discriminatory contract enforcement and dispute settlement?
- Are there efforts underway to identify whether technical codes need to be updated in light of climate change? What support is available to help enable and prioritise these interventions?
- Does land use planning account for the evolution of climate risks over time? Are these planning processes enforced?

Relevant tools and resources

Topic	Resource
Sectoral regulation	FAO-UNDP-UNEP – Repurposing agricultural support to transform food systems OECD – Agricultural Policy Monitoring and Evaluation: adapting agriculture to climate change OECD – Effective Carbon Rates 2023 Global Commission on the Economics of Water – Turning the Tide OECD – Recommendation of the Council on Water OECD – Regional and National Policy Dialogues OECD – Water and Climate Change Adaptation
Technical codes and regulatory norms	CEN-CENELEC – Guidance on Climate change adaptation for infrastructure standards GCA – Stocktake of Climate-resilient Infrastructure Standards GFDRR – Building Reguation for Resilience Infrastructure Canada – Codes, standards and guidance for climate resilience
Economic regulation of infrastructure	UK National Infrastructure Commission – Regulation & Resilience

Box 3.3. Case studies: regulatory alignment to reflect the benefits of climate resilience

Climate-resilient Infrastructure Standards in Canada

Canada has invested in two programmes to support climate resilience for infrastructure and the built environment. These aim to support the development of voluntary standards for climate resilience and inform the development of regulatory codes:

- Climate Resilient Build Environment Initiative (2021-2028) – this CAD 25 million (USD 25 million) programme is led by the National Research Council of Canada and supports research and the development of tailored tools and guidance for a climate-resilient built environment. It includes, for example, research to inform the revision of key standards and codes for bridges to account for climate change impacts.
- Standards to Support Resilience in Infrastructure Program (2021-2026) – this CAD 11.7 million (USD 8.6 million) is led by the Standards Council of Canada and aims to develop new standards and guidance to address climate risks. This programme aims to advance 36 new standards and technical guidance documents and promote the adoption of revised guidance across relevant industries.

Climate Resilient Water Sector in Grenada

Grenada is faced with pressures on its water resources, given rising temperatures, changing patterns of rainfall and saltwater intrusion into groundwater sources due to sea-level rise. The Green Climate Fund (GCF) is supporting efforts to improve water efficiency and management in Grenada with a grant of USD 38.7 million. This project, implemented by GIZ (the German development agency), includes an integrated package of measures that aim to improve water security. These measures include the creation of a Water Resources Management Unit (WRMU) as a national regulator, improvements in data collection and revision of water tariffs to encourage efficiency. Technical and financial support will be provided to the agriculture and tourism sectors to help them improve their efficiency of water use, for example through the use of rainwater harvesting.

Japan's Agricultural Adaptation Plan

Japan's Ministry of Agriculture, Forestry and Fisheries (MAFF) developed its Adaptation Plan in 2015 to address the impacts of climate change on the sector. This aims to precisely and effectively respond to climate change impacts. Necessary measures are mainly arranged and promoted as a plan for each field (e.g. agricultural production, plant pests etc.) and crop (e.g. paddy field rice) for the next ten years. This Plan also aims to help realise potential opportunities brought by climate change, such as the expansion of areas where subtropical and tropical fruits can be cultivated. In cooperation with local governments, MAFF monitors global warming impacts, and has offered information concerning adaptive measure in the annual *Global Warming Impact Investigation Report*.

Source: Government of Canada (2024[38]); GCF (2018[39]); OECD (2023[28]).

Insurance and risk transfer

Insurance and risk transfer arrangements have a critical role in helping to manage the consequences of physical climate risks, as well as raising awareness of climate risks and providing incentives to invest in risk reduction. This building block examines key issues, including the implementation of effective insurance and risk transfer strategies, understanding of risk exposure and support for resilient reconstruction.

Insurance and risk-transfer arrangements have a critical role, given that physical climate risks are a significant driver of investment in climate change adaptation (see Chapter 2). Effective insurance and risk-transfer mechanisms can support greater visibility of climate-related risks, provide incentives to invest in reducing physical climate risks through investments in adaptation and provide a mechanism to support resilient reconstruction (see Box 3.4) (OECD, 2023[40]). The role of risk transfer at the project level is covered in the section on "Support and incentives for private investment".

Countries have developed different systems for managing the financial consequences of extreme events, involving different sets of responsibilities in relation to the public and private sectors. Even where insurance is provided by the private sector, there tend to be significant degrees of government involvement. For example, in the US the National Flood Insurance Program (NFIP) is directly administered by the federal government, while in Australia, France and the UK insurance is offered by private companies who are able to access dedicated reinsurance programmes (OECD forthcoming, 2024[41]). These diverse institutional arrangements, reflecting different national circumstances and priorities, mean that the general principles outlined below will need to be applied in different ways.

At the global scale, increasing the availability of insurance and risk-transfer arrangements supports investment in general (OECD, 2015[26]). In 2023, recorded global losses from extreme weather and climate-related events reached USD 281 billion in that year, yet only 40% of these losses were insured (AON, 2024[42]). Within this average, there is considerable variation between countries. For example, the European Central Bank estimates that only 25% of climate-related catastrophe losses are insured in Europe, but in some European countries this figure is less than 5% (ECB and EIOPA, 2023[43]). Climate change will make it more challenging to provide insurance coverage, as potential losses become larger and less predictable. Ensuring that insurance and risk-transfer mechanisms contribute to risk reduction can help to manage these impacts and support the availability of affordable terms, while also providing an incentive for adaptation investment.

International cooperation has a critical role in expanding access and use of insurance mechanisms in developing countries, including innovative tools such as index insurance and parametric insurance. Developing countries face distinct challenges in expanding insurance, including lack of access to financial services, high transaction costs relative to the value of assets insured and lack of affordability. The G7/V20 Global Shield against Climate Risks initiative was launched in 2023 to provide a comprehensive mechanism to support vulnerable countries to enhance their financial resilience to extreme events (G7-V20, 2023[44]). This can include the provision of technical and financial support to address barriers to insurance coverage. Insurance mechanisms can also be complemented with tools for disaster risk financing including catastrophe bonds bond and contingent credits (Clarke et al., 2016[45]).

Insurance and risk transfer arrangements ought to increase the visibility of physical climate risks. Governments can support this process by (i) undertaking multi-hazard assessments that evaluate direct and indirect climate impacts (ii) promoting the development of technologies and expertise in monitoring and assessing risks across the public, private, and non-profit sectors (iii) ensuring data relevant to understanding disaster impacts is produced and shared publicly (iv) and assessing financial capacities to manage the impacts of disasters across public and private sectors, including the use of risk financing and risk transfer tools (OECD, 2023[40]).

Policies governing insurance markets and risk-transfer arrangements should aim to minimise the potential for "moral hazard" and therefore support investment in risk reduction. This means that insurance premiums should reflect the underlying risk. The OECD's Recommendation on Building Financial Resilience to Disaster Risks calls for ensuring that financial policy, supervision and regulatory arrangements "[enable] pricing, contractual terms and conditions (e.g. premiums, deductibles, coverage limits) that encourage and support risk reduction where relevant and as appropriate" (OECD, 2023[46]). In doing so, reductions in risk from investment in adaptation can translate into reduced insurance premiums.

Governments can also ensure that the policy, regulatory and supervisory framework is conducive to resilient recovery from extreme events. Traditionally, insurance coverage aims for a like-for-like replacement of the damaged asset. However, the reconstruction process can be a critical moment for investing in adaptation, such as raising critical equipment to a higher floor. Mechanisms to encourage resilient recovery include provision of information following an extreme event on options to reduce risks, access to credit and provision of additional coverage to enable additional works following an extreme event. The UK's Flood Re programme's Build Back Better initiative, for example, will reimburse up to GBP 10 000 (EUR 11 700) beyond the cost of a standard repair to fund resilience measures (see Box 3.5).

Where there are challenges in moving to risk-reflective pricing or resilient recovery, governments may consider offering subsidies for risk reduction measures through grants, tax credits, or loans directly to households and businesses facing increasing climate risks (OECD, 2023[40]). For example, in the United States, programmes such as Strengthen Alabama Homes, South Carolina Safe Home and My Safe Florida Home provide grants to policyholders to implement risk reduction measures to protect against hurricane damages. In Queensland, Australia a Betterment Fund was introduced to enable resilient reconstruction for locally owned public assets, such as roads and drainage infrastructure. They estimated that investment of AUD 174 million (EUR 105 million) in betterment has already led to savings of AUD 379.5 million (EUR 230 million) in reduced damage and disruption.

Losses that are not covered by insurance can create liabilities for the public sector and the scale of these liabilities may not be understood prior to a loss occurring. Potential liabilities include (i) the expected costs of relief and recovery, with an emphasis on building back with greater resilience (ii) exposures to losses as a result of funds invested into insurance or guarantees (iii) estimated payments under public compensation and financial assistance (iv) unanticipated demands or needs for public compensation, assistance and/or transfers (v) potential impact of macroeconomic deterioration (OECD, 2023[46]). Developing plans or frameworks to address the impact of climate-related disasters on public finances can help to ensure climate-risks are adequately priced, and all relevant actors across the economy, especially governments, are prepared to respond when climate-related disruptions occur.

Box 3.4 Insurance and the enabling environment for investments in adaptation

The OECD's Investment and Private Pensions Committee has identified the following potential contributions of the insurance sector to supporting investment in adaptation:

- Providing analytics to better understand physical climate risks, using tools such as catastrophe models. These tools can provide probabilistic estimates of the level of climate risk to homes, buildings and public assets in specific locations.
- Sharing expertise to climate policy makers, individual policyholders and wider communities on effective adaptation and risk reduction measures.
- Applying premium pricing that reflects the level of risk to provide a signal of risk exposure and an incentive to reduce risks.
- Funding reinstatement of damaged assets to be more resilient to climate change impacts (also referred to as "build back better").

However, the ability to realise these potential benefits will depend upon having a conducive regulatory environment. An underlying challenge is the short-term nature of insurance contracts, which mean that companies have limited incentive to support risk reduction activities by policyholders (such as "build back better") if the benefits can subsequently be reaped by a competitor.

Source: OECD (2023[47])

Guiding questions

- Do mechanisms exist to help insurers accurately reflect climate risk? What frameworks or standard-setting tools exist to ensure the quality and accuracy of climate-risk assessments across the insurance sector?
- Do mechanisms exist to motivate insurers and other institutional investors to align investments with adaptation and resilience needs? Are there clear incentives for risk reduction and resilience building activities?
- Do governments help to communicate climate risks that cannot be reduced? Are risk-sharing arrangements well-understood among households, businesses, and governments at all levels?
- Does the insurance market offer policies that include resilient recovery from extreme events? Are there market or regulatory barriers to such products?
- Do mechanisms exist to understand the impacts of climate-related disasters on public finances? How do governments account for the costs associated with climate risk, including the ex-ante fiscal costs posed by contingent liabilities?

Relevant tools and resources

Topic	Resource
Initiatives	UNEP – Forum for Insurance Transition to Net Zero IDF – Insurance Development Forum CISL – Climate Wise SMI – The Sustainable Markets Initiative MCII – The Munich Climate Insurance Initiative UNEP FI – The UN Principles for Sustainable Insurance G7/V20 – The Global Shield against Climate Risks
Guidance	ILO – Protecting the Poor: A Microinsurance Compendium OECD – Enhancing the Insurance Sector's Contribution to Climate Change Adaptation OECD – Recommendation of the Council on Building Financial Resilience to Disaster Risks World Bank – Financial Resilience against Climate Shocks and Disasters

Box 3.5. Case studies: Insurance and risk transfer

Public-private insurance initiatives to provide flood insurance in the United Kingdom

"Flood Re" was established by the 2014 Water Act, as a joint initiative between the UK Government and the UK insurance industry. It provides reinsurance for flood risk to a) promote affordability and availability of insurance for UK households at high flood risk and b) to manage the transition to risk-reflective pricing of flood insurance for household premises. It is a not-for-profit fund, owned and managed by the insurance industry. Funding for claims comes from two sources: a charge for each policy that is ceded to Flood Re (determined by the value of the property) and an additional annual levy on UK home insurers, which is currently GBP 135 million (EUR 159 million). In doing so, it provides a cross-subsidy for flood risk. Following the introduction of Flood Re, 80% of homes with previous flood damage saw their insurance premiums fall by at least 50%. To avoid subsidising new development in high-risk areas, this programme only covers properties built before 2009.

Flood Re introduced the first nationwide resilient reconstruction programme in 2022. This enabled up to GBP 10 000 to be reimbursed for resilience measures following a loss event. Following recent storms, Flood Re estimated that 30% of claims included an element of resilient reconstruction.

Sharing climate-risks in large-scale infrastructure projects

In Canada, the Government of the Northwest Territories and the Tłı̨chǫ Government are working in partnership to develop the Tłı̨chǫ All-Season Road project. The 97-kilometre all-season highway is intended to provide uninterrupted access between remote norther communities with the Northwest Territories, even in the face of climate change. The project is jointly funded by the Government of Canada (25%) and the Government of the Northwest Territories (75%). The Tłı̨chǫ All-Season Road project includes a bespoke climate change risk-sharing mechanism that uses modelling of climate risks to effectively price long-term risk exposure for the operations and maintenance of a road constructed above permafrost. In the event climate change impacts exceed the ranges set by the Government, any financial impacts will be shared between proponents to a predetermined cap. The risk-sharing mechanism was developed through the Request for Proposal (RFP) period, which enabled all proponents to effectively price climate risk from the outset.

Parametric insurance: restoring coral reefs in the event of hurricanes

The Mesoamerican Reef (MAR) spans Mexico, Belize, Guatemala and Honduras. An innovative parametric insurance programme, the MAR Insurance Programme, has been introduced to provide insurance coverage to finance restoration of the reef following hurricanes. Insurance coverage is provided by commercial provider, while the programme benefits from financial support from Canada (via the Ocean Risk and Resilience Alliance) and Germany (via the Insuresilience Solutions Fund). Under the policy, insurance claims are paid automatically when certain conditions are met at designated points. As the insurance policy is based on a parametric trigger, payouts can be made quickly following a hurricane. For example, following Hurricane Lisa in 2022, payouts were made within 14 days of the event. This programme has expanded to cover 11 sites along the reef.

Source: Flood Re (2024[48]); CCPPP (2019[49]); Climate Champions (2023[50]).

Public finance and investment

> Critical investments for climate change adaptation lie within the remit of the public sector, including capacity building and some forms of infrastructure. This building block examines the extent to which fiscal policies, budgetary processes and tools are conducive to mainstreaming climate resilience into public spending, while ensuring that sufficient resources are available for public investments in priority areas for adaptation

Climate change will affect budgetary needs and priorities. For example, additional resources may need to be allocated to some areas (e.g. protective infrastructure, provision of climate data) to address climate risks. The relative priority of areas of spending may also change because of climate change. Green budgeting provides a framework that can support the integration of adaptation into budgetary processes. For budget allocations, key instruments include the integration of climate into the design of medium-term expenditure frameworks, requirements specified in the budget preparation phase ("budget circular") and reporting (Blazey and Lelong, 2022[51]). These efforts can be supported by the development of measurement frameworks to define and track public investment that supports climate adaptation. Examples of national approaches to mainstreaming into public finances can be found in Box 3.6

Project and programme appraisal tools need to be fit for purpose for a changing climate, given the role of uncertainty, non-market benefits and discount rates. The UK government has adopted supplementary guidance to support the appraisal of adaptation-related projects. The application of commonly used approaches for appraisal, including cost-benefit analysis and cost-effectiveness analysis, may need to be adjusted to account for these characteristics (OECD, 2015[6]). For example, the benefits of adaptation investments will often include non-market components, such as saving lives, benefits for health or well-being. These benefits can be included through the use of non-market valuation or multi-criteria analysis for project selection. Specialised approaches, such as Real Options Approaches[2], can support decision making when there are significant uncertainties.

Public procurement is another critical area for steering public expenditure towards activities that support adaptation. Integrating climate resilience can increase upfront costs, while generating benefits over the life of the investment. Procurement policies that only consider upfront cost can therefore discourage the selection of more resilient solutions. The use of Life-Cycle Costing can provide a level playing field for resilient investments. Performance standards may also need to be updated to reflect the projected impacts of climate change. In the case of PPPs, risks related to climate change should be clearly identified and allocated, suitable insurance required and provision made for adaptive management (PPIAF, 2016[52]).

On the revenue side, the structure of taxation policies may need to be examined to strengthen incentives for adaptation. Policy options include setting a policy framework that allows for the implementation of taxes or charges on externalities relevant to adaptation. For example, the city of Philadelphia has introduced a stormwater fee based on impermeable surface area, which provides an incentive to replace paved areas with green spaces (US Government, 2024[53]). Tax credits and rebates can be used to encourage retrofitting and investment in R&D (see also below: financial support).

Tracking expenditure relevant to climate change adaptation can increase accountability and transparency. If linked to targets, such tracking can also provide an incentive to mainstream adaptation. UNDP has developed the Climate Public Expenditure and Institutional Review (CPEIR) process to support the identification of climate-relevant expenditure (UNDP, 2015[54]). Several other countries, including France and Germany, have undertaken independent analyses to examine the value of public spending linked to climate change adaptation objectives finding that only a small share of government spending currently contributed to climate change adaptation.

Guiding questions

- Does the process of allocating budgets take into account the potential impacts of climate change?
- Do project or programme appraisal tools account for the benefits of adaptation?
- Do public procurement policies account for benefits over the lifecycle of the investment? Do the systems for asset management aim to optimise costs of existing assets over their lifespans?
- Does the process for allocating risks within PPPs account for climate risks?
- Is there a strategy in place to manage the financial consequences to the public sector of climate extremes?

Relevant tools and resources

Topic	Resource
Green budgeting and mainstreaming into public finances	IMF – Planning and Mainstreaming Adaptation to Climate Change in Fiscal Policy IMF – How to Make the Management of Public Finances Climate-Sensitive–"Green PFM" OECD – Best practices for Green Public Procurement OECD – Climate Change Risks and Adaptation: Linking Policy and Economics OECD – Paris Collaborative on Green Budgeting OECD – Recommendation on Disaster Risk Financing Strategies UK Government – Accounting for the Effects of Climate Change UNDP: Climate Public Expenditure and Institutional Review (CPEIR) Methodological Guidance
Procurement and PPPs	Blue Dot Network – Certification for quality infrastructure GCA – Knowledge Module on PPPs for Climate-resilient Infrastructure IADB – Climate Resilient Public Private Partnerships: A Toolkit for Decision Makers OECD – Going Green: Best Practices for Public Procurement World Bank Group – Climate Toolkits for Infrastructure PPPs

Box 3.6. Case studies: mainstreaming into public finance and investment

Mainstreaming adaptation into the European Union's budget

Climate change is being mainstreamed across the European Union's 2021-2027 Multiannual Financial Framework, which covers EUR 1.2 trillion of planned expenditure, and the EUR 807 billion NextGeneration EU initiative. The EU has committed to ensuring that 30% of total expenditure contributes to climate mitigation and/or adaptation. Beyond this, all expenditure is subject to a "do no harm principle" to ensure that budget expenditure is consistent with the EU's climate and environment goals.

To support the achievement of these targets, the Commission has integrated budget tagging into its core financial systems. The Commission also committed to producing annual reports to outline the share of past expenditure that contributed to climate objectives, as well as estimates of future expenditure. The Commission has also developed tools and guidance to support the application of the "do no harm principle", including dedicated guidance for infrastructure projects.

Climate Toolkits for Infrastructure PPPs

Public-Private Partnerships are an important tool for mobilising investment in infrastructure. From an adaptation perspective, there is both the need to ensure that infrastructure commissioned through PPPs is resilient to climate change, but also an opportunity to use PPPs to support investment in infrastructure that helps to protect against climate change impacts. The World Bank Group has developed a set of Toolkits to support the integration of climate adaptation and mitigation into PPP advisory work and project structuring. It includes an overall toolkit covering general issues, such as risk allocation within PPP contracts, and a series of toolkits for infrastructure sectors that provide more detailed guidance and suggest relevant performance indicators.

Governance for Resilient Development in the Pacific (Gov4Res)

The Governance for Resilient Development in the Pacific programme (Gov4Res) works with local and national governments and regional organisations in the region. The programme aims to mainstream resilient development into the government systems that are responsible for planning, financing and overseeing development. In doing so, it has a particular focus on gender equality and social inclusion. Outputs under this project include the introduction of climate budget tagging in Fiji, Solomon Islands and Tuvalu. It also includes a capacity building component to support the integration of risk informed development into the budget development process. The project is being implemented by UNDP, with funding committed from Australia, Korea, New Zealand, Sweden and the United Kingdom

Source: EC (2022[55]); Neves et al. (2022[56]); UNDP (2024[57]).

Sustainable finance

Sustainable finance instruments can support the allocation of capital to adaptation investments. Increased transparency on climate-related risks can help investment decisions integrate physical climate risks and potential future costs, providing a market signal to better manage relevant risks. This building block examines the arrangements that are in place to realise this potential, including the existence of usable taxonomies, disclosure arrangements and suitable financial instruments.

Financial instruments

There is growing market demand for financial instruments that are intended to contribute to environmental and social objectives, including ESG funds, green, social, sustainability and sustainability-linked bonds (GSSS) (OECD, 2023[58]), and sustainability-linked bonds (SLBs) (OECD, 2024[59]). OECD analysis found that the value of sustainable bonds issued by the corporate sector (including financial and non-financial companies) was six times larger in 2019-23 than in 2014-18. The amount of outstanding sustainable bonds by the corporate sector reached USD 2.3 trillion in 2023, while official sector sustainable bonds reached USD 1.99 trillion (OECD, 2024[60]). Adaptation and resilience, however, currently constitutes a small part of the overall market. Around 19% of GSSS bonds issued in 2022 were identified as having at least some of the proceeds used for adaptation and resilience-related activities.

GSSS bonds encompass two families of instruments, each with different implications for supporting investment in adaptation (OECD, 2024[59]). The first, use-of-proceeds GSSS bonds, are issued to finance specific activities that are intended to deliver environmental or ESG benefits and are not tied to the performance of the issuing entity. Meanwhile, SLBs are linked to the achievement of certain performance thresholds by the issuing entity. SLBs issued have predominantly included performance thresholds linked to mitigation, while the use of adaptation-relevant measures remains very rare (CBI, 2024[61]). Each of these categories has different requirements for investment in adaptation: use of proceeds bonds require a pipeline of projects that can be defined as contributing to climate change adaptation (see below). Expanding the use of SLBs for adaptation will require the development and adoption of relevant performance standards.

The public sector can help to create momentum in markets for green financial instruments that support adaptation. At the national level, for example, France issued EUR 10 billion of Obligation assimilable du Trésor (OAT) vertes (green bonds) in 2023. That same year, EUR 1.98 billion of the proceeds from green bonds were allocated to climate change adaptation (See Box 3.8). In the UK, Green Gilts have raised GBP 2.1 billion (EUR 2.5 billion) for climate change adaptation measures (HMT, 2023[62]). Development banks can also play a critical role in supporting the development of markets for climate-resilient debt instruments. Since 2019, EBRD raised USD 700 million for adaptation investments by issuing a dedicated climate resilience bond (EBRD, 2024[63]). The Asian Infrastructure Development Bank has issued a USD 500 million Climate Adaptation Bond to fund projects that deliver resilience benefits (AIIB, 2023[64]). In September 2023, the Japan International Cooperation Agency (JICA) issued JPY 32 billion (EUR 200 million) of Disaster Resilience Bond (Sustainability Bonds) under the form of Agency bonds (that are non-government guaranteed domestic bonds) to finance its cooperation projects on the theme of Disaster Risk Reduction and Build Back Better in developing countries.

GSSS bonds have institutional and macroeconomic prerequisites that pose obstacles to their use in least developed countries. These bonds are predominantly issued by high-income and emerging economies, with European jurisdictions representing 67% of global official issuance, 54% of issuance by financial corporates and 45% by non-financial corporates (OECD, 2024[60]). In particular, the use of GSSS bonds requires borrowers to have the capacity to take on more debt, sufficiently developed local capital markets and mechanisms for managing exchange rate risk (OECD, 2024[59]). As such, these mechanisms will not always be appropriate for financing adaptation investments.

Labels and taxonomies

Clear and consistent standards are required to define what counts as an adaptation and resilience investment to support the use of financial instruments, provide transparency to market participants and avoid the risk of greenwashing. A growing volume of standards are now available. For adaptation and resilience, these standards tend to be focussed on the processes undertaken rather than the adoption of specific technologies or compliance with performance standards. In general, these standards focus on demonstrating the climate-related risks have been identified and managed, while avoiding harm to people or the environment (Mullan and Ranger, 2022[65]). Ensuring interoperability between standards, whether these standards are voluntary or mandatory, will support market development and reduce transaction costs.

Climate adaptation has been included in the design of most taxonomies. The EU Taxonomy for Sustainable Activities provides process-based criteria for identifying investments that make a significant contribution to climate change adaptation. It also contributes to mainstreaming by requiring that all "green" investments comply with the Do No Significant Harm principle, which includes the requirement to avoid adverse impacts on climate change adaptation. Climate adaptation is also included within the development of some other national taxonomies, including Chile, South Africa (Box 3.8) and the UK (OECD, 2020[66]). In the case of Chile, the taxonomy under development is based on the EU framework but focuses exclusively on "environmentally sustainable activities". This distinguishes it from the approach taken by other taxonomies, such as South Africa's, which includes a broader range of assets, projects, activities, and sectors. For jurisdictions that decide to develop official taxonomies, the G20's Sustainable Finance Roadmap encourages the use of common terminologies, industry classifications and regional interactions to enhance interoperability and support market development (G20 SFWG, 2021[67]).

There is also a growing set of efforts to define adaptation-related investments by non-government actors. Japan updated its guidance on green bonds in 2022 to provide further emphasis on adaptation, Do No Significant Harm and propose relevant key performance indicators (KPIs) for adaptation (Japan Ministry of the Environment, 2022[68]), The Climate Bonds Initiative developed a Climate Bonds Resilience Taxonomy, which aims to provide clear performance standards for adaptation measures (CBI, 2024[69]). Climate change adaptation projects can also be included within bonds that are issued within the International Capital Market Association's Green Bond Principles. Toolkits have been developed to identify investments that have resilience benefits. These include frameworks by the Global Adaptation and Resilience Investment Group, the Adaptation and Resilience Investors Collaborative (ARIC) and Standard Chartered (see Relevant Links and Resources below). Ensuring coherence and interoperability between frameworks will be important to reduce transaction costs and the risk of market fragmentation.

Financial system measures can support efforts to better track finance flows relevant to climate change adaptation. The adoption of taxonomies can provide an incentive for financial actors to identify and demonstrate the contribution of their investments to climate change adaptation, thereby helping to fill this gap in the measurement of private sector flows. New tools, such as AI, have the potential to translate heterogenous corporate disclosures into a better-harmonised understanding of the investments being made that are relevant to adaptation. For example, the Bank for International Settlement has a pilot project to translate disclosure documents into harmonised indicators of climate risk (BIS, 2024[70]).

Disclosure and transparency

The failure to adequately consider climate risks, including physical climate risks, within financial markets can lead to misallocation of capital and the accumulation of risks within the financial system (TCFD,

2017[71]). Initiatives to achieve greater transparency and disclosure within financial markets can support the allocation of capital to investments that are more resilient to climate change (see Box 3.7). The starting point is for entities to disclose climate-related risks. The Taskforce on Climate-related Financial Disclosure (TCFD) recommended the disclosure of physical climate risks. These risks are included in major frameworks for disclosure, including the International Sustainability Standard Board's (ISSB) "IFRS Sustainability Disclosure Standards, S2 Climate-Related Disclosures" (IFRS, 2023[72]) and the European Union's European Sustainability Reporting Standards. The Global Reporting Initiative is currently consulting on updates to the standards for Companies that may voluntarily report on climate-related risks as part of their sustainability commitments.

The effectiveness of disclosure in raising awareness of physical climate risks, and therefore potentially supporting investment in climate-resilience, depends upon the breadth, robustness and usability of the information being reported. An analysis of reporting under the TCFD guidelines found that physical climate risks were included in less than half of the reports. Those organisations reporting risks tended to only feature some potential climate hazards and used different scenarios, metrics and assumptions (Zhou and Smith, 2022[73]). The adoption of common metrics and more detailed guidance for reporting on physical climate risks would facilitate greater transparency in this area (EBRD and GCECA, 2018[74]). For example, the ISO 14091 standard can be used to provide an overall framework for undertaking climate change risk assessments at the organisational level (ISO, 2021[75]).

A critical issue for investment in adaptation is to ensure that mechanisms for disclosure reflect the benefits of adaptation, rather than just looking at potential physical climate risks. An overly narrow focus on risk exposure could have the undesired effect of diverting finance flows away from the areas that are most in need of investment for adaptation. It is also important to have transparency about adaptation efforts, so that the benefits of relevant investments can be considered in decision-making. Transition plans were developed to address an analogous issue for climate mitigation and provide a potential mechanism for providing transparency about how reporting entities plan to adapt to the impacts of a changing climate. The UK's Transition Plan Taskforce's Adaptation Working Group has produced guidance on how adaptation can be integrated within transition plans (See Box 3.8)

Box 3.7. Integration of climate resilience and project cashflow

Ensuring that a project is well adapted to climate change may increase upfront costs. These costs can arise, for example, from increased project preparation time due to the need to understand how the project will be affected by climate change risks. They may also arise from the cost of technical changes required to manage climate risks, such as specifying materials that can handle hotter temperatures. These upfront costs should be outweighed by the benefits over the lifetime of the project: these benefits can include lower insurance premiums, lower operating costs and reduced risk of premature obsolescence.

Well-functioning financial markets should reflect these benefits in the valuation of financial assets, thereby encouraging investment in adaptation. However, information asymmetries can prevent these benefits from being correctly priced, thereby discouraging investment in adaptation.

Figure 3.1. Stylised model of how mainstreaming climate resilience can affect project cashflow

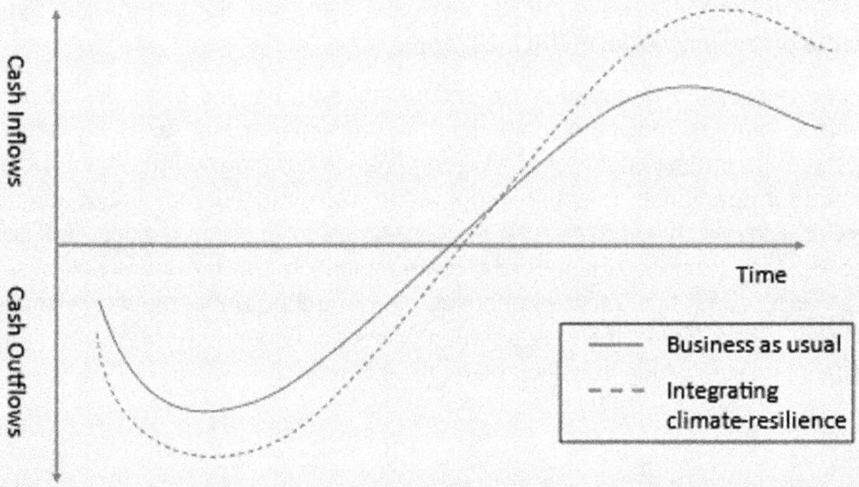

Source: OECD (2024[29]) based on CCRI (2021[76])

Guiding questions

- Are there voluntary or mandatory standards/mechanisms or principles for identifying adaptation investments that have been adopted by market participants? How is compliance with those standards/mechanisms or principles measured and verified?
- Are mechanisms in place to provide transparency about the exposure of financial assets to physical climate risks? What guidance exists to support disclosure in relation to the choice of metrics, scenarios and assumptions?
- Do requirements for corporate disclosure, including transition plans, address adaptation? Do these reflect the benefits of adaptation, as well as exposure to physical climate risks?
- Is there a taxonomy for green and sustainable finance? If so, does this taxonomy include criteria for climate resilience?
- Is there any technical or financial support available for potential issuers of climate resilience financial instruments?

Relevant tools and resources

Topic	Resource
Disclosure	EBRD and GCECA - Advancing TCFD Guidance On Physical Climate Risks And Opportunities EU – European Sustiainability Reporting Standards GRI – Project for Climate Change Standards ISSB – Sustainability Disclosure Standards TCFD - Recommendations of the Task Force on Climate-related Financial Disclosures
Transition plans	OECD - Guidance on Transition Finance EIB – Paris Alignment for Counterparties (PATH) UK Transition Plan Taskforce – Building Climate-ready Transition Plans
Taxonomies	Climate Bonds Initiative – Climate Bonds Resilience Taxonomy Methodology EU - Taxonomy for Sustainable Activities ICMA – Green Bond Principles ICMA - Sustainability-linked Bond Principles Intact Centre – Climate Risk Matrices
Private sector and voluntary initiatives	IIGCC – Working Towards a Climate Resilience Investment Framework GARI – Climate Resilience Investments in Solutions Principles Standard Chartered, KPMG and UNDRR – Guide for Adaptation and Resilience Finance UNEP FI – Adaptation & Resilience Impact: A measurement framework for investors UNEP FI – Climate Adaptation Target Setting BII and FMO – Climate Investment Playbook

Box 3.8. Case studies: sustainable finance

French Sovereign Green Bonds ("OAT vertes")

France was one of the first countries to issue a sovereign green bond ("*obligations assimilables du Trésor verte*") in 2017. Since then, France has issued further sets of green bonds, reaching a total value of EUR 61.9 billion by the end of 2023. The proceeds from these bonds are allocated to eligible green expenditures for climate change mitigation, adaptation, biodiversity and efforts to reduce pollution. This issuance is compatible with the French system for green budgeting, with almost all eligible expenditures from the green bonds being rated in the budget system as environmentally favourable (or, at a minimum, neutral). To ensure transparency and environmental integrity, an independent council has been established to evaluate the performance and allocation of these green bonds and the issuances are verified by an independent third party.

The proportion of green bond receipts allocated in support of climate change adaptation has increased over time, reaching EUR 1.98 billion (19% of the EUR 10.2 billion of eligible expenses that year). The majority of these funds are used for capacity building, data and research (including satellite observation), bilateral cooperation and contribution to transversal projects.

Guidance on integrating climate change adaptation into private sector transition plans

The UK's Transition Plan Taskforce was launched in 2022 to develop a framework for companies to disclose their plans for transitioning their operations towards a low-carbon, climate resilient future. The focus of transition plans has largely been in relation to making the transition to net zero, but the UK's guidance also included climate change adaptation. This recognised that companies will also have to adapt to physical changes resulting from climate change. The Taskforce commissioned dedicated guidance on integrating adaptation into transition plans and has integrated the insights from this guidance into the core Framework and dedicated sectoral guidance documents, with the aim of encouraging disclosing entities to also discuss their plans for adaptation. The International Financial

Reporting Standards (IFRS) Foundation has now taken responsibility for the disclosure-related materials produced by the Transition Plan Taskforce.

South Africa's Green Finance Taxonomy (GFT)

South Africa released a Green Finance Taxonomy (GFT) in 2022 to provide a tool for identifying "green" assets, projects, activities and sectors, based on international good practice and national requirements. The Taxonomy was developed by the South African National Treasury. The development of the taxonomy was supported by the International Finance Corporation (IFC), with support from Sweden and Switzerland. This taxonomy follows the structure and approach of the EU Taxonomy, with the aim of achieving interoperability. It includes climate adaptation as an environmental objective and process-based criteria for identifying activities that contribute to this objective.

Source: Agence France Tresor (2023[77]); TPT AWG (2024[78]); SA National Treasury (2022[79]).

Support and incentives for private investment

> Barriers to private investment in adaptation include low perceived or actual returns on investment and an inability of the private sector to capture the full social benefits generated by adaptation investments. These barriers are compounded by the double externality effect associated with climate innovation in the case of new adaptation technologies. Addressing these market failures can help strengthen incentives for adaptation investments. This building block covers support for climate-resilient investment projects (e.g. tax incentives, project preparation facilities, incubators, etc.) and measures to mitigate risks associated with adaptation investments (e.g. guarantees, concessional loans).

Private investment in adaptation includes direct investment into firm and supply chain resilience or into the provision of adaptation solutions, and financing of adaptation investments of others through corporate or project finance (see Chapter 2). The private sector does not necessarily internalise the positive spillovers of adaptation finance and investments, nor the full physical climate risks that the investments are intended to address. Targeted support by the government may therefore be warranted to support innovation and adaptation investments that deliver wider social benefits. Different forms of support will apply to direct investors and financers. Financial incentives (e.g. tax breaks, grants) and non-financial incentives (e.g. regulatory incentives, technical and business support) can alleviate barriers faced by direct investors. De-risking instruments (e.g. guarantees, concessional finance), while also available to direct investors, can be particularly helpful to mitigate the risks that inhibit institutional investors and banks from providing finance for adaptation projects. Project preparation helps financers identify bankable projects, while providing support to project developers. More tailored forms of support are needed to address the challenges associated with adaptation innovation.

Incentivising direct investments

Incentives for adaptation investments, whether financial or non-financial, should be targeted and cost-effective. They should be complementary to a sound policy framework for investment and cannot compensate for a weak regulatory environment (OECD, 2015[26]).

Investment tax incentives can target adaptation investment by increasing related after-tax profits, reducing costs associated with certain expenses or exempting recipients from indirect taxes. Existing incentive schemes in sectors that have clear links to climate change adaptation could be revised to integrate adaptation considerations and impact metrics. For example, the Government of Peru introduced a mechanism in 2008 that allowed private firms to prepay a portion of their income taxes in the form of public works to reduce Peru's infrastructure gap. Through this mechanism, private companies assume the upfront costs and management of new infrastructure programs while the government accepts the infrastructure projects in lieu of future tax payments. Adaptation considerations could be integrated into such incentive schemes by ensuring the climate resilience of new infrastructure.

Tax incentives can be very costly in terms of foregone revenues, create market distortions, or result in windfall gains for investments that would have materialised also in the absence of the incentive regime. Cost-based regimes that are linked to specific expenses and inputs have the potential to mobilise more investment per unit of forgone tax revenue than profit-based incentives (Clark and Skrok, 2019[80]). According to the OECD Policy Framework for Investment and FDI Qualities Toolkit, incentive regimes should be time-limited, well-targeted and subject to regular review, and their uptake and cost-effectiveness should be regularly monitored and evaluated. The OECD is currently in the process of developing a comprehensive checklist to assist governments in crafting, executing, managing, and assessing investment incentives, which strives to ensure that these incentives effectively support sustainable development objectives (including adaptation) while addressing any associated costs.

Non-financial incentives also have an important role to play in encouraging adaptation investments, by reducing the administrative burden and time costs of an investment project. For instance, investment promotion agencies (IPAs) can work to streamline investment processes, provide revenue guarantees for strategic projects, form or facilitate joint ventures and support site visits. Invest India works closely with multiple ministries and agencies to address bottlenecks for climate mitigation FDI, including navigating the national approval system for environmental assessments and land acquisition for larger projects. Establishing a clear mandate for the IPA to support climate adaptation investments can help tailor IPA efforts and resources to alleviating administrative processes associated with adaptation investments, and provide advisory services to ease market entry and support the operations of prospective investors (OECD, 2022[81]; WEF, 2023[82]).

Mitigating risks to project finance

The strategic use of public resources can enhance access to finance and help to address the perception that investments in adaptation are too risky relative to the return that they are likely to deliver. It can also help to address short-termism in decision-making and raise awareness. For example, the state-owned Development Bank of Japan offers loans at favourable rates to enterprises based on their ratings in terms of disaster prevention and business continuity management. By 2022, USD 3.9 billion of loans had been extended under this programme (OECD, 2023[20]).

More generally, a range of instruments can be used to enable enterprises to access finance on more favourable terms (Table 3.2). These include government guarantees, equity stakes, concessional debt finance and blended finance[3] in the case of developing countries (OECD, 2021[83]). These instruments can be delivered through different institutional arrangements, including multilateral institutions (such as the European Investment Bank), national development banks, specialised public or private green investment banks and development partners (see Box 3.9 for the example of PIDG). Local financial institutions can be used as intermediaries to provide access to credit on concessional terms to small and medium-sized enterprises (SMEs). Providing these institutions with a mandate to support adaptation efforts can encourage a greater focus on supporting this type of investment. The role of insurance against physical climate risks is covered in the section on “Insurance and risk transfer”.

Government guarantees are a sovereign obligation to protect the beneficiary from defined losses if specified conditions occur and can help make adaptation projects more acceptable to private investors. At the same time, government guarantees expose governments to fiscal risks due to the difficulty of predicting when guarantees are called and the size of the payout. Guarantees should therefore be carefully structured to provide only the minimum to make projects bankable. This entails coverage of a limited number of specific risks that depend on the types of projects, sources of financing, and the political, economic, and financial market conditions of the host countries (IBRD, 2019[84]).

Non-sovereign cross-border guarantees have the potential to make a significant contribution to mobilising adaptation finance in emerging markets and developing economies (EMDEs). Such guarantees are typically provided by multilateral development banks, development finance institutions, export credit agencies, or specialised institutions (i.e. private sector institutions funded by governments and development partners). A recent mapping of cross-border guarantees found that out of 52 existing guarantee instruments, only five are designed to mitigate risks associated with adaptation finance (CPI, 2024[85]). These guarantees are typically provided by specialised institutions like GuarantCO and the Green Guarantee Company, and focus on de-risking green bonds and loans.

The OECD Guidance on Blended Finance for Adaptation report identifies good practices for scaling-up adaptation finance via blended finance. It identifies opportunities for using blended finance in key sectors including agrifood, infrastructure, health and nature and biodiversity. It also outlines the following principles for ensuring the effective use of blended finance in this context (OECD, 2024[19]):

- Optimise blended finance for adaptation objectives based on a development rationale.
- Consider risk of development reversals in the absence of adaptation when assessing additionality.
- Focus on opportunities to use blended finance for the integration of adaptation into the domestic financial sector.
- Pursue blended finance for adaptation with a focus on scale, standardisation and systemic solutions.
- Use systematic high-quality adaptation data in a dynamic climate change process.

Table 3.2. Types of de-risking instruments

Category	Instrument	Description
Equity stakes	Co-investment	Project-level equity provision by a public actor alongside private investors
	Cornerstone stake	Majority stake equity investment by a public actor in a fund to attract other investors
	Subordinated equity	Junior equity provision by a public actor to a fund to minimise losses to private investors
	Public seed capital	Concessional fund allocation using public money
Concessional debt	Co-financing	Project-level debt provision by a public actor alongside private financiers
	Loan	Debt issuance by a public actor
	Subordinated debt	Junior debt provision by a public actor
	Shareholder loan	Loan provided by a public actor while an existing shareholder
Facilities	Credit facility	A rolling line of credit by a public actor
	Liquidity facility	A facility by a public actor allowing the borrower to draw thereupon in case of cash flow shortfall
Guarantees and insurance	Loan guarantee	Guarantee by a public actor to pay any amount due on a loan in the event of non-repayment
	Revenue guarantee	Guarantee by a public actor to purchase a product to ensure revenue cash flow for a project
	Backstop guarantee	Guarantee by a public actor to purchase any remaining equity shares if they go unsold
	Investment insurance	Guarantee by a public actor to indemnify in case of investment losses
	Political risk insurance	Guarantee by a public actor to indemnify in case of political risks (e.g. expropriation)

Source: Adapted based on OECD (2021[83])

Supporting project preparation

The project development phase is needed to translate worthwhile concepts into high-quality, effective and financially viable projects. This phase provides an entry point for understanding the characteristics of the project and linking the requirements for different funding sources. It follows on from the identification of priority needs (section 3.1). This phase can represent an additional hurdle to investments in climate change adaptation, because of the need for technical capacity to understand climate risks and the potential complexity of developing projects that deliver multiple co-benefits. The smaller average size of adaptation projects relative to mitigation projects can make individual projects unattractive to potential investors.

Support for capacity development as a public good can underpin the development of investments in adaptation. A key area for this is the open provision of data, tools and guidance for managing climate change risks (see Building Block 1 for more on this). Peer-learning mechanisms can also provide a source of inspiration and support in translating project proposals into implementation.

Project preparation facilities (PPFs) can provide an important contribution to help translate concepts into implementation. There are a wide range of PPFs, with varying sectoral and geographic coverage. For example, the Global Infrastructure Facility (GIF) was established by the G20 to support the preparation of sustainable infrastructure projects. The current landscape of PPFs is fragmented and existing PPFs often have limited private sector involvement. Greater coordination and pooling of efforts could help achieve scale and increase project take-off. Governments can support their effectiveness by encouraging greater collaboration between PPFs and harmonisation of documents and processes (EC HLEG, 2024[86]). The development of country platforms could facilitate this process of collaboration and help to avoid gaps and reduce duplication of efforts.

For countries eligible to receive climate finance, capacity constraints can hinder the development of projects that meet the funders' requirements. At the international level, the Green Climate Fund provides support for project preparation through its project preparation facility, with a simplified process available for grants of less than USD 300 000. The Adaptation Fund provides grants of up to USD 50 000 to assist with Project Formulation. National climate funds, such as Rwanda's Green Fund (FONERWA), can rationalise access to climate finance, provide a central source of expertise with the requirements of different funding sources and support project development (OECD, 2023[20]).

The use of intermediaries and programmatic approaches can help to unlock access to private investment. For example, the Urban Resilience Fund B (TURF) uses a blended finance approach to combine private capital, with support from public development banks to fund infrastructure in Africa. The use of intermediaries can provide greater flexibility to adjust application requirements to the scale of the project.

Fostering innovation and technology transfer

New technologies can improve adaptative capacity and increase resilience to climate change. For example, risk modelling firms are using new analytical capabilities provided by artificial intelligence (AI) and machine learning to develop risk scores for future climate conditions that can be integrated into insurance products (OECD, 2023[40]). Supplier tracking systems that combine internet-of-things sensors and AI are being used to reroute the distribution of healthcare products based on current environmental conditions (The White House, 2024[87]). Deep learning techniques are being exploited to design drought-resistant crops at the molecular level (WEF, 2024[88]). Breakthrough innovations, defined as having higher potential societal impact and higher scientific novelty than incremental innovations, have the potential to make especially large contributions to building climate resilience.

Innovative technologies and solutions emerging from R&D must pass through several stages of validation and refinement before reaching full commercialisation. Due to long development timelines, high technology risks (especially high for climate technologies), and information asymmetries, adaptation technologies are vulnerable to funding gaps (OECD-World Bank-UN Environment, 2018[89]). Generally, R&D in breakthrough technologies relies more heavily on public support, as this is where the risk is highest and commercial viability is most remote. Private sector firms generally fund less risky R&D to improve the performance, reduce the costs of existing products, or build on the results of publicly funded early-stage efforts (UNFCCC, 2017[90]). Once the technology is developed, recent evidence suggests that traditional venture capital models may not be well-suited to funding demonstration and early-stage commercialisation of climate adaptation technologies, due to the relatively poor risk-return profile of such investments (Gaddy et al., 2017[91]). Scaling breakthrough innovations may be especially risky because it is unknown how markets will react to them.

Governments can help address some of these challenges through a variety of support measures affecting the supply and demand for breakthrough innovations in climate adaptation (Table 3.3). These include directly investing in R&D (or subsidising private R&D), expanding incubators and accelerators to support commercialisation of new technologies, investing in technical and data infrastructure, promoting inter-disciplinary collaborations across academia and industry, investing in skills and training, and providing regulatory exemptions to facilitate testing of innovations. The public sector also plays a key role in promoting knowledge-sharing on what constitutes effective adaptation and resilience building. Demonstration of resilient investments and best practices is a form of knowledge-sharing that can further stimulate technological innovation as new investors become aware of resilient investment opportunities (World Bank-GFDRR, 2021[92]).

Table 3.3. Measures to support adaptation innovation

Constraint	Policy measures	Examples
Research & development costs and risks	Public R&D, subsidies, tax credits, public venture capital	In Denmark, the Green Tax Reform provides relief for firms investing in R&D and innovation for climate technologies. In France, the "Crédit d'impôt innovation" programme enables SMEs to benefit from tax credits for the creation of innovative solutions, thereby adding economic value to R&D activities. The 30% tax credit applies to expenditure of up to €400,000 per year, which automatically limits it to €80,000 per year per SME.
Demonstration, commercialisation & scaling	Tech start-up support (e.g. incubators, accelerators)	The European Innovation Council (EIC) was established in 2021 to support game changing innovations throughout the lifecycle, from early-stage research to proof of concept, technology transfer, and scale up.
Technical infrastructure	Investment in research, testing and demonstration infrastructure	Testing and Experimentation Facilities for AI co-funded by the EU and Member States to support AI developers that provide a combination of physical and virtual facilities to test AI-based technologies.
Skills and capabilities	Training, international skills attraction	The High-Tech Human Capital Fund in Israel provides grants funding up to 70% of the costs of training programmes focused on advanced technological fields such as quantum, AI, and climate tech.
Cross-disciplinary collaboration	Academic spin-off platforms	Collaborative Laboratories (CoLABs) in Portugal were launched in 2017 to create an interface between academia and industry and increase knowledge transfer and co-creation in key strategic sectors. There are currently 35 COLABS, each including at least one company and one public R&D partner. Carnot label is a French public programme to support partnered research between public laboratories and firms looking for innovative solutions. The Clim'adapt Carnot Institute, which is operated by CEREMA, is a specific program to support bilateral contract research services for adaptation innovation. Since 2020, 16 projects have been successfully led with firms.
Market creation	Public procurement, public-private partnerships, regulatory sandboxes	France Expérimentation allows for regulatory exemptions to facilitate testing of innovation projects including an irrigation solution to fertilise crops reusing wastewater.

Source: adapted from OECD (2023[93])

Small enterprises play an important role in technological innovation but are constrained by weak entrepreneurial support systems, fragmented linkages to climate technology markets, and lack of finance. Incubators and accelerators play an important role in addressing these challenges and strengthening the national innovation ecosystem. They facilitate linkages between entrepreneurs, other innovation actors, suppliers, buyers, and sources of finance. Public support for creating local adaptation-focused innovation centres can help leverage the specialised expertise of firms and universities, while facilitating access to regulatory agencies and financing institutions, as is the case for Kenya's Climate innovation Center. There are estimated to be around 2 000 technology incubators and 150 accelerators worldwide. Public sector is increasing its supports to these centres, as shown by the recent funding of the National Science Foundation (NSF) Colorado-Wyoming Climate Resilience Engine (CO-WY Engine), an accelerator focused on climate resilience technologies that has received a public grant of USD 160 million over the next ten years to help start-ups accelerate R&D for adaptation solutions. However, fewer than 70 are estimated to be climate technology incubators and accelerators, and just 25 of the 70 are in developing countries (UNFCCC, 2018[94]). Limited information is currently available on the specific challenges and opportunities for incubators and accelerators to support innovation in adaptation technologies.

International climate finance can support adaptation innovation by fostering partnerships with businesses on the cutting edge of climate adaptation innovation. For example, the Global Environment Facility's (GEF) Challenge Program for Adaptation Innovation seeks to catalyse adaptation innovation by engaging directly with leading innovators through calls for proposals. After their selection, winning projects are developed and implemented in partnership with one of the 18 GEF agencies. This model of linking directly with ideas of innovation leaders can help engage a broader spectrum of actors in presenting and developing GEF-financed initiatives.

International technology transfer mechanisms and development co-operation have an important role to play in ensuring that innovation benefits a larger number of countries. Technology transfer plays an especially significant role in supporting adaptation efforts of SMEs in emerging economies that that lack access to climate finance (OECD, 2023[95]). International mechanisms have been established to support North-South and South-South technology diffusion, such as the UNFCCC's Technology Mechanism, implemented through the UNEP Climate Technology Centre & Network, which promotes the accelerated transfer of environmentally sound technologies for low carbon and climate resilient development at the request of developing countries.

Guiding questions

- Are existing incentives to stimulate private investment in support of adaptation well-targeted and time-limited? Are measures in place to assess their cost-effectiveness?
- What resources are available to help project developers understand the climate-related risks that they face and potential adaptation measures?
- What support is available to help with early-stage project development? Is climate resilience systematically considered within existing mechanisms for supporting project preparation?
- Are there support mechanisms in place to assist with access to climate finance, such as national climate funds?
- To what extent is the existing intellectual property framework conducive to promoting investment in adaptation innovation and transfer of adaptation technologies among firms?
- What support is available for early-stage innovation in adaptation? Are knowledge transfer facilities in place (e.g. technology centres, business incubators, applied research centres) to provide knowledge exchange and innovation services for adaptation technologies?

Relevant tools and resources

Topic	Resource
Toolkits and guides	EU Climate-ADAPT Platform Japan – Guide for Adaptation Finance OECD – Strengthening capacity for climate action in developing countries US – U.S. Climate Resilience Toolkit US EPA – Water Resiliency and Finance Center OECD – Policy Framework for Investment OECD – FDI Qualities Policy Toolkit OECD – Guidance on Blended Finance for Adaptation (forthcoming) WEF – Guidebook on Facilitating Climate FDI World Bank – Climate Change Knowledge Portal World Bank & UNDRR – Enabling Private Investment in Climate Adaptation & Resilience
De-risking instruments	IBRD – Government Guarantees for Mobilizing Private Investment in Infrastructure CPI – Landscape of Guarantees for Climate Finance in EMDEs Global Centre on Adaptation – Green Bonds for Climate Resilience – A Guide for Issuers NAP Global Network – Inventory of Innovative Financial Instruments for Adaptation
International project preparation facilities (PPFs)	Asian Development Bank – Asia Pacific Project Preparation Facility Asian Infrastructure Investment Bank – Project Preparation Special Fund European Bank for Reconstruction and Development – Infrastructure Project Preparation Facility Green Climate Fund – PPF Global Infrastructure Facility Public-Private Infrastructure Advisory Facility Cities Climate Finance Leadership Alliance – Directory of urban project preparation facilities
Innovation and technology transfer	OECD, Word Bank, UNEP – Financing Climate Futures OECD – Navigating green and digital transitions: Five imperatives for effective STI policy UNFCCC – Climate Technology Incubators and Accelerators UNFCCC – Technology Mechanism UNEP – Climate Technology Centre & Network (CTCN) WEF – Innovation and Adaptation in the Climate Crisis: Technology for the New Normal

Box 3.9. Case studies: support for private investment

Blended finance for infrastructure: the Private Infrastructure Development Group

The Private Infrastructure Development Group (PIDG) was established in 2002 to mobilise private finance for infrastructure in developing countries, with a particular emphasis on least developed countries and fragile states. It is currently supported by six bilateral donors and the International Finance Corporation. It uses concessional finance to mobilise private capital for infrastructure investments, using the following tools across the infrastructure lifecycle:

- Technical assistance for feasibility studies, project incubation and other early-stage activities;
- Project Development to share risks of early-stage project development with other sponsors;
- Credit Solutions including long-term debt, provision of guarantees and credit enhancement facilities.

PIDG estimates that it has mobilised USD 25 billion in private investment for infrastructure since its creation. In 2023, 65% of the PIDG projects contributed to climate change mitigation and/or adaptation objectives.

National support for Climate Resilience initiatives.

In the **United States**, as part of the Inflation Reduction Act (IRA) programme and, on the basis of the National Climate Resilience Framework, the national government has invested USD 3.9 million to encourage private sector players to innovate in the field of climate resilience. The funds were allocated to the National Oceanic and Atmospheric Administration (NOAA) that selected several accelerator programs, which are responsible for screening and selecting the businesses to receive government financial support and technical assistance for ocean-based climate resilience innovations. As a result of this public funding, 16 business accelerators were established and recruited new cohorts of innovative Climate Resilient businesses ideas.

France 2030 is a national investment plan aimed at fostering innovation in the French private sector. The programme deploys ER 54 billion of public investment in various sectors, including improving the resilience of the agricultural sector to the effects of climate change. As a result, a call for proposals entitled 'Agri-food resilience and capacity 2030' was launched and managed by the French public investment bank BPI France, which invested a total of EUR 1.8 billion and selected 357 innovative projects, some of which increase the resilience of the agri-food sector. The funding is specifically designed to support investment in R&D or infrastructure construction.

Egypt's Nexus of Water, Food and Energy (NWFE) Programme seeks to mobilise concessional development finance for climate adaptation in key sectors. This is realised through the design, structuring and preparation of concrete and implementable projects to enhance small farmers' adaptation to climate risks, increase crop yields and irrigation efficiency to build resilience of vulnerable regions, establish early warning systems, and modernise on-farm practices.

Source: PIDG (2024[96]); UNFCCC (2023[97]); US National Science Foundation (2024[98]); Ministry of Agriculture and Food (2024[99]); White House (2024[100]); Egypt Ministry of International Cooperation (2022[101]).

References

ADB (2023), *Climate Adaptation Investment Planning*, https://www.adb.org/publications/climate-adaptation-investment-planning-brochure. [21]

Adshead, D. et al. (2022), *Ghana: Roadmap for resilient infrastructure in a changing climate*, Ministry of Environment, Science, Technology & Innovation, Accra, Ghana, https://gca.org/reports/ghana-roadmap-for-resilient-infrastructure-in-a-changing-climate/. [18]

Agence France Tresor (2023), *OAT VERTES RAPPORT D'ALLOCATION ET DE PERFORMANCE 2022*, https://www.aft.gouv.fr/files/medias-aft/3_Dette/3.2_OATMLT/3.2.2_OATVerte/OAT_2022_FR_FINAL_01_WEB.pdf (accessed on 23 April 2024). [77]

AIIB (2023), *AIIB Issues First Climate Adaptation Bond Targeting Resilient Infrastructure*, https://www.aiib.org/en/news-events/news/2023/AIIB-Issues-First-Climate-Adaptation-Bond-Targeting-Resilient-Infrastructure.html. [64]

AON (2024), *2024 Climate and Catastrophe Insight*, Aon Insurance, https://assets.aon.com/-/media/files/aon/reports/2024/climate-and-catastrophe-insights-report.pdf (accessed on 23 August 2024). [42]

BIS (2024), *Project Gaia: Enabling climate risk analysis using generative AI*, https://www.bis.org/publ/othp84.htm (accessed on 24 October 2024). [70]

Blazey, A. and M. Lelong (2022), "Green budgeting: A way forward", *OECD Journal on Budgeting*, https://doi.org/10.1787/dc7ac5a7-en. [51]

Buurman, J. and V. Babovic (2016), "Adaptation Pathways and Real Options Analysis: An approach to deep uncertainty in climate change adaptation policies", *Policy and Society*, Vol. 35/2, pp. 137-150, https://doi.org/10.1016/j.polsoc.2016.05.002. [102]

Cabinet of Germany (2024), *KLiVO Portal*, https://www.klivoportal.de/EN/Home/home_node.html. [12]

Cançado, D. and M. Mullan (2020), "Stocktake of Climate-resilient Infrastructure Standards", Global Centre on Adaptation. [36]

CBI (2024), *Climate Bonds Resilience Taxonomy Methodology*, Climate Bonds Initiative, https://www.climatebonds.net/resilience (accessed on 24 October 2024). [69]

CBI (2024), *Sustainability-linked Bonds: Building a High Quality Market*, Climate Bonds Initiative, https://www.climatebonds.net/files/reports/cbi_slb_report_2024_04d.pdf (accessed on 23 August 2024). [61]

CCPPP (2019), *The Canadian Council for Public-Private Partnerships 2019 National Award Case Studies: Tłı̨chǫ All-Season Road Project*, https://www.pppcouncil.ca/getmedia/c0c63a91-29b6-4dfb-b4d0-f470d84a2106/2019-Award-Case-Study-Tlicho-Road-final-web.pdf (accessed on 16 August 2024). [49]

CCRI (2021), *THE PHYSICAL CLIMATE RISK ASSESSMENT METHODOLOGY (PCRAM) Guidelines for Integrating Physical Climate Risks in Infrastructure Investment Appraisal*, https://resilientinvestment.org/pcram/ (accessed on 30 April 2024). [76]

CFMCA (2023), *Strengthening the Role of Ministries of Finance in Driving Climate Action: A Framework and Guide for Ministers and Ministries of Finance*, The Coalition of Finance Ministers for Climate Action, Washington D.C., https://www.financeministersforclimate.org/workstream-thematic-reports. [3]

CFMCA (2022), *Strategies for Mainstreaming Climate Action in Ministries of Finance: Governance, Capacities, and Research Practices*, Coalition of Finance Ministers for Climate Action, Washington D.C., https://www.financeministersforclimate.org/news/hp2-publishes-report-mainstreaming-climate-action-ministries-finance. [2]

Cimato, F. and M. Mullan (2010), "Adapting to Climate Change: Analysing the Role of Government", *Defra Working Papers*, No. 1. [27]

Clarke, D. et al. (2016), "Evaluating Sovereign Disaster Risk Finance Strategies A Framework", *Policy Research Working Paper*, World Bank Group, https://documents1.worldbank.org/curated/en/430111468184437717/pdf/WPS7721.pdf (accessed on 3 October 2024). [45]

Clark, W. and E. Skrok (2019), *The Use of Corporate Tax Incentives : A Guidance Note and Experience from Poland, Hungary and Latvia*, World Bank Group, http://documents.worldbank.org/curated/en/180801564468287868/The-Use-of-Corporate-Tax-Incentives-A-Guidance-Note-and-Experience-from-Poland-Hungary-and-Latvia. [80]

Climate Champions (2023), "How innovative insurance solutions are protecting Mesoamerican reefs and communities", *Race to Resilience*, https://climatechampions.unfccc.int/how-innovative-insurance-solutions-are-protecting-mesoamerican-reefs-and-communities/. [50]

CPI (2024), *Landscape of Guarantees for Climate Finance in EMDEs*, https://www.climatepolicyinitiative.org/publication/landscape-of-guarantees-for-climate-finance-in-emdes/. [85]

Delta Programme (2023), *Now for the Future: 2024 National Delta Programme*, https://english.deltaprogramma.nl/documents/publications/2023/09/19/delta-programme-2024-english (accessed on 24 July 2024). [22]

EBRD (2024), *EBRD's Green Bond Issuance*, https://www.ebrd.com/work-with-us/sri/green-bond-issuance.html. [63]

EBRD and GCECA (2018), *ADVANCING TCFD GUIDANCE ON PHYSICAL CLIMATE RISKS AND OPPORTUNITIES*, https://www.physicalclimaterisk.com/media/EBRD-GCECA_draft_final_report_full.pdf (accessed on 4 December 2023). [74]

EC (2022), "Climate Mainstreaming Architecture in the 2021-2027 Multiannual Financial Framework", *COMMISSION STAFF WORKING DOCUMENT*, No. SWD(2022)225, https://commission.europa.eu/document/download/968be999-7fd5-45ac-8c1b-0c9edcce2c15_en (accessed on 16 August 2024). [55]

EC HLEG (2024), *Final recommendations of the High-Level Expert Group on scaling up sustainable finance in low-and middle-income countries*, https://international-partnerships.ec.europa.eu/scaling-sustainable-finance-low-and-middle-income-countries-high-level-expert-group_en#recommendations (accessed on 1 May 2024). [86]

ECB and EIOPA (2023), *Policy options to reduce the climate insurance protection gap: Discussion paper*, https://www.ecb.europa.eu/pub/pdf/other/ecb.policyoptions_EIOPA~c0adae58b7.en.pdf (accessed on 25 July 2024). [43]

Flood Re (2024), *The Quinquennial Review July 2024*, https://www.floodre.co.uk/wp-content/uploads/Flood-Re_QQR-2024_Digital.pdf (accessed on 16 August 2024). [48]

G20 SFWG (2021), *G20 Sustainable Finance Roadmap*, https://g20sfwg.org/wp-content/uploads/2021/10/G20-Sustainable-Finance-Roadmap.pdf (accessed on 24 July 2024). [67]

G7-V20 (2023), *The Global Shield against Climate Risks*, https://www.globalshield.org/. [44]

Gaddy, B. et al. (2017), "Venture Capital and Cleantech: The wrong model for energy innovation", *Energy Policy*, Vol. 102, pp. 385-395, https://doi.org/10.1016/j.enpol.2016.12.035. [91]

GCEW (2023), *Turning the tide: A call to collective action*, https://turningthetide.watercommission.org/ (accessed on 4 July 2024). [32]

GCF (2021), *Readiness proposal with UNDP for the Republic of Tunisia*, Green Climate Fund, https://www.greenclimate.fund/document/national-adaptation-plan-advancing-risk-informed-development-and-land-use-planning-tunisia (accessed on 23 August 2024). [37]

GCF (2018), *Funding Proposal: FP 059: Climate-Resilient Water Sector in Grenada (G-CREWS)*, Green Climate Fund, https://www.greenclimate.fund/sites/default/files/document/funding-proposal-fp059-giz-grenada.pdf (accessed on 20 August 2024). [39]

GCF/NDC (2023), *Partnership Climate Investment Planning and Mobilization Framework*, https://ndcpartnership.org/sites/default/files/2023-12/gcfndc-partnershipclimate-investment-planning-and-mobilization-frameworkconsultation-draft.pdf (accessed on 24 July 2024). [8]

Government of Canada (2024), "Codes, standards and guidance for climate resilience", *Housing, Infrastructure and Communities Canada*, https://housing-infrastructure.canada.ca/climate-resilience-climatique/codes-standards-normes-guidances-eng.html. [38]

Hain, L., J. Kölbel and M. Leippold (2022), "Let's get physical: Comparing metrics of physical climate risk", *Finance Research Letters*, Vol. 46, p. 102406, https://doi.org/10.1016/j.frl.2021.102406. [15]

HMT (2023), *UK Green Financing Allocation and Impact Report*, https://www.dmo.gov.uk/media/egjbgaop/pr280923.pdf (accessed on 23 April 2024). [62]

IBRD (2019), *Government Guarantees for Mobilizing Private Investment in Infrastructure*, World Bank, https://ppp.worldbank.org/public-private-partnership/sites/ppp.worldbank.org/files/2020-02/Government-Guarantees%20for%20Mobilizing%20Private%20Investment%20in%20Infrastructure.pdf. [84]

IFRS (2023), *IFRS S2 Climate-related Disclosures*, https://www.ifrs.org/issued-standards/ifrs-sustainability-standards-navigator/ifrs-s2-climate-related-disclosures/ (accessed on 24 October 2024). [72]

IPCC (2022), *Climate Change 2022: Impacts, Adaptation and Vulnerability*, Cambridge University Press, Cambridge, UK and New York, USA. [30]

ISO (2021), *ISO 14091:2021*, https://www.iso.org/standard/68508.html (accessed on 24 October 2024). [75]

Japan Ministry of the Environment (2022), *Green Bonds and Sustainability-Linked Bonds Guidelines*. [68]

Ministry of Agriculture and Food (2024), *France 2030: the interactive map of award-winners in agriculture and food*, https://agriculture.gouv.fr/france-2030-la-carte-interactive-des-laureats-dans-lagriculture-et-lalimentation (accessed on 3 October 2024). [99]

Ministry of International Cooperation (2022), *Nexus of Water, Food, and Energy Programme*, https://moic.gov.eg/page/nwfe. [101]

Mullan, M. and N. Ranger (2022), "Climate-resilient finance and investment: Framing paper", *OECD Environment Working Papers*, No. 196, OECD Publishing, Paris, https://doi.org/10.1787/223ad3b9-en. [65]

Neves, P. et al. (2022), *Climate Toolkits for Infrastructure PPPs*, World Bank Group, http://documents.worldbank.org/curated/en/099120004052270615/P1746330d584ff0210a9670dcf49a5becb0 (accessed on 16 August 2024). [56]

OECD (2024), *Blended Finance for Adaptation*, OECD. [19]

OECD (2024), *Global Debt Report 2024: Bond Markets in a High-Debt Environment*, OECD Publishing, Paris, https://doi.org/10.1787/91844ea2-en. [60]

OECD (2024), *Infrastructure for a Climate-Resilient Future*, OECD Publishing, Paris, https://doi.org/10.1787/a74a45b0-en. [29]

OECD (2024), *Measuring Progress in Adapting to a Changing Climate: Insights from OECD countries*, OECD Publishing, Paris, https://doi.org/10.1787/8cfe45af-en. [24]

OECD (2024), *Regional and National Policy Dialogues on Water*, https://www.oecd.org/en/networks/regional-and-national-policy-dialogues-on-water.html. [35]

OECD (2024), "Sustainability-Linked Bonds: How to make them work in developing countries, and how donors can help", *OECD Development Perspectives*, No. 44, OECD Publishing, Paris, https://doi.org/10.1787/7ca58c00-en. [59]

OECD (2023), *Agricultural Policy Monitoring and Evaluation 2023: Adapting Agriculture to Climate Change*, OECD Publishing, Paris, https://doi.org/10.1787/b14de474-en. [28]

OECD (2023), "Climate adaptation: Why local governments cannot do it alone", *OECD Environment Policy Papers*, No. 38, OECD Publishing, Paris, https://doi.org/10.1787/be90ac30-en. [4]

OECD (2023), "Enhancing the insurance sector's contribution to climate adaptation", *OECD Business and Finance Policy Papers*, No. 26, OECD Publishing, Paris, https://doi.org/10.1787/0951dfcd-en. [10]

OECD (2023), “Green, Social and Sustainability Bonds in Developing Countries: The case for increased donor co-ordination”, *OECD Development Perspectives*, No. 31, OECD Publishing, Paris, https://doi.org/10.1787/1cce4551-en. [58]

OECD (2023), “Navigating green and digital transitions: Five imperatives for effective STI policy”, *OECD Science Technology and Industry Policy Papers*, Vol. 162, https://doi.org/10.1787/dffb0747-en. [93]

OECD (2023), *Net Zero+: Climate and Economic Resilience in a Changing World*, OECD Publishing, Paris, https://doi.org/10.1787/da477dda-en. [47]

OECD (2023), *OECD Guidelines for Multinational Enterprises on Responsible Business Conduct*, OECD Publishing, Paris, https://doi.org/10.1787/81f92357-en. [5]

OECD (2023), *OECD Guidelines for Multinational Enterprises on Responsible Business Conduct*, OECD Publishing, Paris, https://doi.org/10.1787/81f92357-en. [95]

OECD (2023), “Recommendation of the Council on Building Financial Resilience to Disaster Risks”, *OECD/LEGAL/0436*, https://legalinstruments.oecd.org/en/instruments/OECD-LEGAL-0436. [46]

OECD (2023), *Scaling Up Adaptation Finance in Developing Countries: Challenges and Opportunities for International Providers*, Green Finance and Investment, OECD Publishing, Paris, https://doi.org/10.1787/b0878862-en. [20]

OECD (2022), *FDI Qualities Policy Toolkit*, OECD Publishing, Paris, https://doi.org/10.1787/7ba74100-en. [81]

OECD (2021), “Biodiversity, natural capital and the economy: A policy guide for finance, economic and environment ministers”, *OECD Environment Policy Papers*, No. 26, OECD Publishing, Paris, https://doi.org/10.1787/1a1ae114-en. [31]

OECD (2021), “De-risking institutional investment in green infrastructure: 2021 progress update”, *OECD Environment Policy Papers*, No. 28, OECD Publishing, Paris, https://doi.org/10.1787/357c027e-en. [83]

OECD (2020), *Common Ground Between the Paris Agreement and the Sendai Framework : Climate Change Adaptation and Disaster Risk Reduction*, OECD Publishing, Paris, https://doi.org/10.1787/3edc8d09-en. [10]

OECD (2020), *Developing Sustainable Finance Definitions and Taxonomies*, Green Finance and Investment, OECD Publishing, Paris, https://doi.org/10.1787/134a2dbe-en. [66]

OECD (2018), *Making Blended Finance Work for the Sustainable Development Goals*, OECD Publishing, Paris, https://doi.org/10.1787/9789264288768-en. [103]

OECD (2016), “Recommendation of the Council on Water”, *OECD Legal Instruments*, https://legalinstruments.oecd.org/en/instruments/OECD-LEGAL-0434. [34]

OECD (2015), *Climate Change Risks and Adaptation: Linking Policy and Economics*, OECD Publishing, Paris, https://doi.org/10.1787/9789264234611-en. [6]

OECD (2015), *Policy Framework for Investment, 2015 Edition*, OECD Publishing, Paris, https://doi.org/10.1787/9789264208667-en. [26]

OECD (2014), *Climate Resilience in Development Planning: Experiences in Colombia and Ethiopia*, OECD Publishing, Paris, https://doi.org/10.1787/9789264209503-en. [1]

OECD (2013), *Water and Climate Change Adaptation: Policies to Navigate Uncharted Waters*, OECD Studies on Water, OECD Publishing, Paris, https://doi.org/10.1787/9789264200449-en. [33]

OECD forthcoming (2024), *The design of flood risk insurance programmes*. [41]

OECD-World Bank-UN Environment (2018), *Financing Climate Futures: Rethinking Infrastructure*, OECD Publishing, Paris, https://doi.org/10.1787/9789264308114-en. [89]

PCAST (2023), *Extreme Weather Risk in a Changing Climate: Enhancing prediction and protecting communities*, President's Council of Advisors on Science and Technology, https://www.whitehouse.gov/wp-content/uploads/2023/04/PCAST_Extreme-Weather-Report_April2023.pdf (accessed on 19 August 2024). [16]

PIDG (2024), *2023 Sustainability and Impact Report*, https://cms.pidg.org/wp-content/uploads/2024/07/PIDG-2023-Annual-Sustainability-and-Impact-report-Final-Digital.pdf. [96]

PPIAF (2016), *Climate Risks and Resilience in Infrastructure PPPs: Issues to be Considered*, https://library.pppknowledgelab.org/attached_files/documents/2870/original/PPIAF_ClimateResilience_IssueBrief.pdf?1458848137 (accessed on 5 March 2018). [52]

Roston, E. et al. (2024), *The Risky Business of Predicting Where Climate Disaster Will Hit*, Bloomberg Green, https://www.bloomberg.com/graphics/2024-flood-fire-climate-risk-analytics/?utm_source=website&utm_medium=share&utm_campaign=copy (accessed on 19 August 2024). [14]

SA National Treasury (2022), *South African Green Finance Taxonomy: 1st Edition*, https://www.treasury.gov.za/comm_media/press/2022/SA%20Green%20Finance%20Taxonomy%20-%201st%20Edition.pdf (accessed on 22 August 2024). [79]

TCFD (2017), *Recommendations of the Task Force on Climate-related Financial Disclosures i*, https://www.fsb-tcfd.org/wp-content/uploads/2017/06/FINAL-TCFD-Report-062817.pdf (accessed on 21 February 2018). [71]

The White House (2024), *The Climate Resilience Game Changers Assessment*, https://www.whitehouse.gov/wp-content/uploads/2024/07/Climate-Resilience-Game-Changers-Assessment.pdf. [87]

TPT AWG (2024), *Building Climate-ready Transition Plans: A primer for preparers*, https://transitiontaskforce.net/adaptation/ (accessed on 1 May 2024). [78]

UNDP (2024), "Governance for Resilient Development in the Pacific", *Transparency Portal*, https://open.undp.org/projects/00120330. [57]

UNDP (2023), *New partnerships to accelerate much-needed investment for climate adaptation*, https://climatepromise.undp.org/news-and-stories/new-partnerships-accelerate-much-needed-investment-climate-adaptation. [9]

UNDP (2015), *Climate Public Expenditure and Institutional Review (CPEIR) – Methodological Note*, https://www.undp.org/asia-pacific/publications/climate-public-expenditure-and-institutional-review-cpeir-methodological-note (accessed on 24 July 2024). [54]

UNFCCC (2023), *Good practices and lessons learned on the setup and implementation of National Systems of Innovation*, https://unfccc.int/ttclear/tec/NSI.html. [97]

UNFCCC (2022), *Navigating the landscape of support for the process to formulate and implement national adaptation plans*, https://unfccc.int/sites/default/files/resource/2022_ac_navigating.pdf. [11]

UNFCCC (2018), *Climate Technology Incubators and Accelerators*, Bonn: United Nations Framework Convention on Climate Change, http://www.unfccc.int/ttclear/incubators. [94]

UNFCCC (2017), *Enhancing financing for the research, development and demonstration of climate technologies*, https://unfccc.int/ttclear/docs/TEC_RDD%20finance_FINAL.pdf. [90]

UNFCCC LEG (2023), *National Adaptation Plans 2023: UNFCCC LDC EXPERT GROUP PROGRESS IN THE FORMULATION AND IMPLEMENTATION OF NAPs*, https://unfccc.int/sites/default/files/resource/NAP-progress-publication-2023.pdf (accessed on 24 April 2024). [7]

US Government (2024), "Stormwater Billing", *Philadelphia Water Department*, https://water.phila.gov/stormwater/billing/. [53]

US National Science Foundation (2024), *Colorado-Wyoming Resilience Engine*, https://www.co-wyengine.org/ (accessed on 3 October 2024). [98]

van Buuren, A. (2019), "The Dutch Delta Approach", in *Great Policy Successes*, Oxford University PressOxford, https://doi.org/10.1093/oso/9780198843719.003.0011. [23]

WEF (2024), *Innovation and Adaptation in the Climate Crisis: Technology for the New Normal*, https://www3.weforum.org/docs/WEF_Innovation_and_Adaptation_in_the_Climate_Crisis_2024.pdf. [88]

WEF (2023), *Guidebook on Facilitating Climate FDI*, https://www3.weforum.org/docs/WEF_Guidebook_on_Facilitating_Climate_FDI_2023.pdf. [82]

White House (2024), *Catalyzing American Innovation in Climate Resilience*, https://www.whitehouse.gov/ceq/news-updates/2024/07/25/catalyzing-american-innovation-in-climate-resilience/ (accessed on 3 October 2024). [100]

White House (2023), *National Strategy to Develop Statistics for Environmental-Economic Decisions*, https://www.whitehouse.gov/wp-content/uploads/2023/01/Natural-Capital-Accounting-Strategy-final.pdf. [25]

World Bank (2024), *Climate Change Knowledge Portal for Development Practitioners and Policy Makers*, https://climateknowledgeportal.worldbank.org/. [13]

World Bank (2024), *The Nature-Based Solutions Opportunity Scan: Leveraging Earth Observation Data to Identify Investment Opportunities in NBS for Climate Resilience in Cities and Coasts across the World*, https://hdl.handle.net/10986/41725 (accessed on 25 July 2024). [17]

World Bank-GFDRR (2021), *Enabling Private Investment in Adaptation and Resilience*, https://doi.org/10.1596/35203. [92]

Zhou, L. and P. Smith (2022), *Physically Fit? How Financial Institutions Can Better Disclose Climate-Related Physical Risks in Line with the Recommendations of the TCFD*, https://www.wri.org/research/physically-fit-financial-institutions-climate-recommendations-tcfd (accessed on 10 February 2023). [73]

Notes

[1] The Producer Support Estimate (PSE) measures all transfers to agricultural producers individually. It includes the net effect of Market Price Support (MPS), which represents transfers from taxpayers and consumers to agricultural producers through domestic prices that are higher than their international reference prices. It also includes budgetary support direct from taxpayers.

[2] Real Options Approaches provide a means of accounting for the value of flexibility when making decisions (Buurman and Babovic, 2016[102]).

[3] Defined as the strategic use of development finance for the mobilisation of additional finance towards sustainable development in developing countries (OECD, 2018[103]).

4 Towards increased investment in adaptation

This chapter provides an overview of the key themes for the Climate Adaptation Investment Framework. It explores how the components of the Framework can be implemented and identifies potential areas of future work to help overcome barriers to investment in adaptation.

This Framework was developed to identify the domestic policies that can accelerate the pace and increase the scale of investments in climate change adaptation. Signs of the need to shift from business-as-usual are already evident: growing difficulties securing insurance coverage in some regions, "extreme" weather events becoming increasingly frequent and increasing costs from weather related events. Proactive, targeted investments in the near-term will reduce future losses and avoid the need for costly and disruptive retrofitting. It is likely that investments in adaptation will need to increase from the tens of billions of dollars per year to the hundreds of billions of dollars per year.

The need for a step change increase in adaptation investment is also being recognised at the international level, including through the on-going discussions about the New Quantified Collective Goal (NCQG) under the UNFCCC process. The G20's agenda on reform of the Multilateral Development Banks has emphasised the need to increase financing capacity and enhance the mobilisation of private capital (G20 Brazil, 2024[1]). These international efforts, including the provision of concessional finance, will be critical to support adaptation investment in developing countries.

The rapid growth of investment in clean energy provides a positive example of how a strong and supportive policy framework, innovation and private capital can have transformative impact in unlocking investment. There has been a virtuous cycle: supportive policy environments drove investment, investment drove unit costs down through innovation and learning-by-doing, and lower costs have made it easier to invest. A similar effort is now needed to strengthen the enabling environment for adaptation to help drive the transformation needed to enhance resilience.

The elements needed to underpin these efforts are emerging, ranging from initiatives to support adaptation planning to the development of taxonomies for climate adaptation. There is increasing engagement from key actors including governments, private sector, philanthropies, and international organisations. Yet, overall, there are significant data gaps and uneven implementation of measures to strengthen the enabling environment. This Framework has been developed to be iterative and pragmatic, drawing upon international good practices where these are available and highlighting issues that governments should be considering as they seek to strengthen the enabling environment.

Translating this Framework into a stronger enabling environment at the national level will often require additional guidance and support. For each of the "building blocks", links to additional resources and support are provided. Beyond this, the sequencing and prioritisation of reforms will depend upon country context, based on a comprehensive view of capacities and needs. Country reviews, such as the OECD's Investment Policy Reviews, can provide a valuable mechanism for developing policy recommendations based on the Framework outlined here.

In addition to supporting implementation directly through country engagement, the OECD intends to support the development of this Framework through further analytical and policy work to strengthen the evidence base, reflect recent developments and provide more detailed guidance on specific topics included in the framework. Some of the potential areas include:

- Sequencing and prioritisation of efforts to strengthen the policy enabling environment, reflecting differences in country circumstances and the specific needs of developing countries. This could cover, for example, the interaction of policy reform with capacity and financing constraints and further work to identify the pre-requisites for different financing instruments and strategies. It could also explore the specific needs of different types of private sector actors, including Small and Medium-Sized Enterprises (SMEs).
- Successful approaches to integrating adaptation investment into national planning processes, learning from efforts to implement adaptation investment plans.
- Scalable models for financing investments in climate resilience, including public and private finance sources. This could examine issues such as the development of common metrics for the benefits

of adaptation investments, innovative financing models and policy needs for different types of private sector firms.

References

G20 Brazil (2024), *Communique from the Third G20 Finance Ministers and Central Bank Governors Meeting*. [1]

www.ingramcontent.com/pod-product-compliance
Lightning Source LLC
Chambersburg PA
CBHW061224240926
51846CB00006B/1345
* 9 7 8 9 2 6 4 9 9 8 9 6 4 *